GETTING TO KNOW:

TWENTY TANGO ORCHESTRAS

David Thomas

TANGO JOURNEY

Editors: Mike Stocks, Marion Greenwood
Graphic Designer & Photographer: Adrian Cubitt
Cover art: Marion Greenwood

Thanks and acknowledgements:

First of all to Marion, who is my tango. I count my daily blessings.

To those who have guided my thoughts and words in the creation of this book, with particular gratitude and respect to Michael Lavocah (UK) and Christian Tobler (Switzerland) for their generous technical advice and personal support.

To all in the tango scene, from centuries past to the present, who have added to the magic.

And finally, to you, for choosing to get to know Twenty Tango Orchestras. I hope that you enjoy it.

CONTENTS

PART FOUR: THE COMPLEX

Appendices

The Author

Introduction

We love to listen and dance to the music of the great tango orchestras, but why should we get to know the people playing the music?

We do not have to, of course, but increasing our knowledge of them also increases our sense of connection. When I was growing up in Liverpool in the 1960s I listened, unsurprisingly, to the Beatles and to many other 'Mersey Beat' groups and singers in the charts at that time. I had their pictures on my bedroom wall, I read interviews and stories about them in the music press, and in my own way I felt that I knew them. Whenever I listened and danced to their music, I could visualise them playing and, subconsciously, I knew who they were and what they were like. In my mind, this connected me more closely to the music. I have tried to achieve the same with the tango orchestras, without the posters in my bedroom.

The orchestra leaders that you will meet in the following chapters did not appear from nowhere – they were part of a continuum of tango musicians that had emerged in the nineteenth century. Their music changed as the years went by and so we should recognise that their 'orchestra' was never a single entity of musicians fixed for the duration of their recording history but often had several formations each with a distinct sound and style.

The singers and musicians too had their own stories before joining the orchestras with which they are most commonly associated and several went on to form their own orchestras at the end of the main dance period, during the 1950s. For example, from the Caló musicians came the orchestras of Francini-Pontier, Maderna, and Federico; from D'Arienzo came that of Varela; from Firpo came Cambareri; and from Troilo came Basso and Piazzola. Singers that went on to develop solo careers included Castillo, Vargas, and Fiorentino.

Some of the individuals and orchestras that we will meet have had more influence than others in the tango dance genre, and today some are more frequently played than others. I have not made comparisons between them nor deliberately assigned more prominence to some over others. The intention is that we get to know them all and then we can each have our own opinions and preferences.

Similarly, there are some recordings that are regarded much more highly than others (whether for technical brilliance, danceability, sound production, or simply sheer enjoyment). The recordings that I refer to, and are included in the recommended playlist, are not a selection of 'The Best of Orchestra x'. I have chosen them to demonstrate a particular aspect of the sound, whether an instrument, a voice, or a change of style.

You will see that the construction of the book has four Parts: *The Simple*, *The Rhythmic*, *The Lyrical* and *The Complex*.
The categories are not intended to narrowly define the variety of the music nor the versatility of the orchestras, but to ease your journey through the information.

The Simple
The music is easy to listen to, follow, anticipate and dance to. It has a steady tempo with few counter-melodies and little decoration.

The Rhythmic
All music has rhythm, but I use the term 'Rhythmic' to bring to mind the sensation of a short, sharp drumbeat (known as the *staccato* style).

The Lyrical
The music emphasises softer emotions created by the use of smooth and flowing notes (known as the *legato* style).

The Complex
The music has many component parts, delivering counter-melodies and decorations in a changing tempo. Complex does not necessarily mean difficult, but can initially present challenges to unfamiliar ears and feet.

Each Part comprises chapters covering the different orchestras, and within each chapter there are four sections: *Personal Story*; *Signature Sounds*; *Singers*; *Musicians*.

The idea of the book is that you, the reader, get to know the orchestras in your own way, and not necessarily in my way. It is not important whether you take on board the book's structure and content completely, or challenge it and come to different conclusions. I hope it is as though we are discussing a mutual friend, and you say, "I know what you mean, but I see him/her differently".

You may prefer to think of Donato as 'Rhythmic' rather than 'Simple', for example, or you may identify a style of playing that differs from the four categories I use. We all hear music differently, so a romantic lyrical tango to one listener may be a rhythmic tango to another. What really matters is that we each know how the music sounds to our own ears.

Additionally, the style and characteristics of the orchestras changed over the years, and even over decades in some cases. Here we are getting to know them mainly during the time that they burst on to the tango dance scene and produced their most emblematic recordings - the tangos that are most frequently played at milongas. But at the same time we are acknowledging that as the years went on they adapted their sound –

usually by slowing down and placing more focus on the singer.

How to get the best from the book:

I recommend that you read the chapters whilst having on-line access to our website www.tango-journey.com where you can listen to all of the recommended tracks on our YouTube Channel playlist. You can also browse a selection of photographs of all of the orchestra leaders and many of the singers and musicians. You will also find a number of tango film clips that are referred to throughout the book.

PART ONE:
THE SIMPLE

Francisco Canaro

Personal Story

Francisco Canaro was born in 1888, not in Buenos Aires, nor elsewhere in Argentina, but in Uruguay, to Italian immigrant parents whose family name was Canarozzo. His father was a civic administrator during an unsettled political time that resulted in an armed revolution when Francisco was only nine years old. Within the next year or two the family fled across the Río de la Plata, where the now rapidly maturing Francisco experienced his family's decline in to extreme poverty.

Francisco was a hard working boy and young man. He was driven to make money in order to avoid the humiliating poverty that he had endured with his parents in his childhood. He took work wherever he could find it. At one point he was painting the woodwork of the newly built Congressional Palace. Whether or not he knew it at the time, also wielding a paintbrush there was Roberto Firpo.

Most probably Canaro would have been successful in any area of work, but it just happened that very early on he started to make money by playing an instrument – a crude violin-like instrument whose body was made from an old olive oil can. He was pushy, he was good at playing a passable tune, he enjoyed himself, and most importantly he collected a few pesos for his efforts.

He also had the fortune of good timing – it was 1900, and here he was, still a boy, getting involved in a new wave of popular music and mixing with the early pioneers, such as his neighbours the Greco brothers.

His drive to succeed in every way possible produced innovation for decades to come. He credits himself with introducing new aspects to the sound, structure and composition of the tangos we now take for granted, such as: the concept of an *estribillista* (the singer coming on just to deliver the second chorus and then off again); the descriptive name 'orquesta típica' for those specialising in the tango sound; and the introduction of the musical form 'milonga' as we now know it.

As a somewhat difficult character, Canaro has many negative labels attached to him. He was nicknamed by musicians as the Kaiser – presumably reflecting his overbearing, probably bullying nature. He was regarded by many as a populist, playing and recording anything as long as the pay was good. The latter criticism may have been true, but was certainly not unique to him, and could equally apply to Lomuto, Donato, OTV, Firpo, D'Arienzo, and Rodríguez.

What cannot be taken away from Canaro is that he was a self-made success (both financially and culturally). He established and chaired SADAIC, the organisation to protect copyright for tango composers and lyricists (although this is likely to also have been a case of poacher turned gamekeeper). He was extremely generous to his family – ensuring his parents never wanted for anything again, looking after his brothers, particularly Humberto, Rafael, Juan, and Mario by buying them instruments and getting them in to the tango business in Buenos Aires and Europe, and financially supporting his sister Rosa who was widowed with five children. Francisco was also notably generous to his musicians and friends, giving them large loans to get them through difficult times. Most important of all, however, is that he produced a wealth of beautiful and danceable music (tangos, valses, and milongas) that we still love to dance to today.

He is credited with composing many favourites such as *El Chamuyo* (also recorded by Donato and OTV); *La Tablada* (also recorded by Donato and Troilo); *Nobleza De Arrabal* (also recorded by Di Sarli, Troilo and Pugliese); and *Nueve Puntos* (recorded by Di Sarli).

His first recording was in Brazil in 1915 and the last in November 1964, the month before he died.

Signature Sounds

Canaro recorded for a period of five decades and so it is to be expected that his style changed. However, he was much more active than the other orchestra leaders in his experimental variations.

Although he was recording prior to the 1920s, the earliest tangos we hear today are from 1925 and give us the flavour of the sound of the 'Old Guard' *orquesta típica criollo*. Listen to:
 * *Organito de la Tarde* (1925).

It was at the same time that the De Caro orchestra (who you will meet soon) introduced the more complex sound known as the 'New Guard'. In response Canaro released his *orquesta sinfóni*ca recordings from 1929 to 1933 and, following their great success, adopted the fuller orchestral sound.

In 1937, as a response to the innovative success of Roberto Firpo, he created his own quintet (named Don Pancho) solely for the recording studios. Listen to:
 * *Duelo Criollo* (1939).
In 1940 he changed the quintet name to Pirincho but the recordings were to become less attractive to the dancer.

Along the way Canaro had a tendency to surprise and delight us with unusual guest instruments.

During the late 1920s to the start of the 1930s, for example, he introduced the slide guitar. Listen to:

   * *Sin Rumbo* (1931)

In the 1930s his inspiration was drawn from North American Jazz (in which he had dabbled from 1923 to 1927, recording under the name of the Canaro Jazz Band) and that brought us woodwind and brass. One common signature sound for Canaro is the clarinet. Listen to:

   * *Te Quiero Todavía* (1939)

Hearing woodwind is an immediate notification that the tango is probably Canaro. But his close friend Francisco Lomuto had a clarinetist in his orchestra too, and had a style similar to Canaro. So how can you be sure it is Canaro and not Lomuto? One way is to listen for the presence of Lomuto's signature sounds – if they are absent then you can be sure you are listening to Canaro. There is more on Lomuto in the next chapter.

Canaro is often kind to us and leaves us in absolutely no doubt that it is him by adding the main signature sound that is brass, in the shape of the trumpet. Go no further, this is Canaro. Listen to:

   * *Recuerdos de Paris* (1937)

The clarinet and trumpet stay with Canaro through the 1930s, 40s, and 50s.

In the 1940s, having recorded tangos for over twenty years, he introduced another surprise signature sound – the organ. Again, once it kicks in you can be sure this is Canaro. Listen to:

   * *Corazón Encadenado* (1942)

This track, like many others, incorporates more than one identifying sound and in this case the trumpet can be heard in the background until it breaks cover in the closing seconds.

Singers

Canaro recorded with many singers for different commercial markets: radio, cabaret, theatre, film, discs, and the dance halls (milongas). Amongst them were household names such as Ada Falcón, Nelly Omar, and Tita Merello, but our focus is trained on his singers for the dance market – and then only those that we dance to most in our twenty-first century milongas.

We can start as far back as 1927 with the voice of Agustín Irusta. When these tracks are played at milongas today they sound like the earliest raw days of tango, but we should remember that by this time Canaro had been recording tangos for twelve years already, and playing for longer still.

Agustín Irusta was from an age before individual microphones, and so on these tracks his voice is projected through a megaphone, which was the best way to compete with the musicians all pushing their sounds down a single acoustic receiver! Even as technology progressed Irusta preferred, now as a matter of style rather than necessity, to sing through a megaphone. He recorded about eighty tracks with Canaro from 1927 to 1932. Listen to:
 * *Alma Tanguera* (1927)

In the same period, Canaro recruited a young cinema fan Carlos José Perez Urdinola. His stage name was Charlo, in tribute to his all-time hero Charlie Chaplin. Charlo's height of fame and influence with Canaro occurred from 1928 to 1931, when he recorded about six hundred tracks, but he recorded tangos with others as early as 1925 and as late as 1967. Listen to:

   * *Canto Por No Llorar* (1931)

Canaro was forever restless and looking for the next great innovation to maintain and grow his public appeal. In about 1930 he changed his style to a bigger sound – his symphonic period – and he needed a different type of singer. A popular name at the time was Ernesto Famá, who had already recorded with the sextets of Osvaldo Fresedo and Carlos Di Sarli, and with the Orquestas Típicas Victor and Porteña.

Famá's popularity was based not just in his singing but also in his rapport with the audience. He looked good and he brought in the crowds. Canaro's primary motivation, it seems, was not artistic expression but mass appeal, and Famá brought him an established following.

Famá was a showman and took care to look immaculate for his fans. One of Canaro's musicians described how the singer would never sit down between numbers for fear of creasing his trousers. He stayed with Canaro from 1930 to 1934, before returning again five years later. Listen to:

* *Todo Te Nombra* (1939)

Having completed the year 1934 with a brief stint by a singer called Carlos Galan, in 1935 Canaro changed his style of singer again with the Italian-born Roberto Maida. Maida had travelled throughout Europe and worked with many of the great tango pioneer names. He had even sung at The Savoy Hotel in London, where the Prince of Wales reportedly played a decent tango on the bandoneón!

Maida sounds more mature than Famá, calmer and 'breathier' in style. He recorded some two hundred tangos with Canaro. Listen to:

* *El Adiós* (1938)

In 1938 Canaro was on the move again, looking for something different to stay ahead in the popular ratings. He wanted a second singer to offer a contrasting sound, and so he introduced Francisco Amor to the orchestra. Maida found this intrusion in to his territory too difficult and walked away from his contract with Canaro, his artistic sensibilities offended.

Amor recorded just over twenty tracks with Canaro from 1939 to 1941. You can see him two years earlier, performing a number in the 1937 film *'Viento Norte'*. He appears at about the forty-eighth minute. Listen to:

* *Cuartito Azul* (1939)

The unexpected departure of Maida left Canaro with a second singer but no first singer. He brought back the popular Ernesto Famá, who worked very well alongside Amor. In fact they worked so well together that they frequently went touring for short spells, leaving Canaro without any singer, and then they left him permanently in 1941.

Canaro recruited the well-known and highly regarded Carlos Roldán who went on to record about ninety tracks from 1941 to 1945. But the orchestra leader still preferred two singers on his team, and so he organised a competition to find one on a Radio Belgrano programme (incongruously sponsored by Palmolive Soap). The inexperienced singer Eduardo Adrián won, and went on to record some thirty-five tracks from 1941 to 1943. You can hear him in *Tango Brujo* (1943).

From November 1944 to April 1946 Canaro recorded with Guillermo Coral – who was already an established stage, radio, and film singer – performing under his real name of Guillermo Rico. You can watch him perform in the 1943 film *'El Fabrica de Estrellas'*, at about the eleven-minute mark. His particular talent was to mimic the style of other singers, and Canaro later remarked that he was never really sure whether his recording voice was his own or not.

There are many more Canaro singers that we could mention, but will not – a reminder that this book is an introductory guide rather than an encyclopaedia. We will conclude with just one more.

Canaro was once again recruiting and Juan D'Arienzo recommended a singer calling himself Alberto Guida. After auditioning him, Canaro took him on and very soon gave him the name Alberto Arenas, after a character in a play. Arenas stayed from 1945 to the mid 1950s. Listen to:

* *La Melodía de Nuestro Adiós* (1947)

Musicians

Canaro's musicians are as many and as varied as his recording years and discography, and so it is difficult to pinpoint individuals on particular recordings. Dozens of them made transient appearances, often returning several times over the years for a particular recording session, broadcast or performance. Canaro's 430-page autobiography *Mis Memorias* does not help us, with his musicians receiving little mention due, he says, "to the tyranny of lack of space". However there were a few long-serving regulars.

The unsung hero of the Canaro orchestra was his trusted pianist, Luis Riccardi, who was there from as far back as 1918 right through to the early 1940s. The piano is not an overtly obvious part of the Canaro sound, but Riccardi played a vital and constant role as Canaro's right-hand adviser and musical arranger. The early days were difficult for Riccardi, whose initial musical style was more aligned to the complexity of the De Caro orchestra, and he was criticised by the Canaro fans that preferred the simpler creole style of his predecessor José Martinez. However, Riccardi learnt quickly and became a much-loved feature of the orchestra in all of its guises over the decades. His stature was evident by 1925, when Canaro went on his grand European tour - it was Riccardi that headed the Buenos Aires Canaro Orchestra in his absence. He also composed many numbers for Canaro, the best known today being the much-played *La Milonga de Mis Tiempos*.

Lead bandoneonist Minotto Di Cicco was with Canaro, on and off, from 1918 to the mid 1920s, returning more substantially in 1932 for the remainder of Canaro's finest dance period including as the sole bandoneonist in Canaro's quintets 'Don Pancho' and 'Pirincho'. Canaro had the highest regard for Minotto's mastery of the instrument, and was particularly taken with his invention of an extra large bandoneón powered by electricity that sounded like a church organ. Listen to:

  * *Invierno* (1937) at about 24 seconds

Alongside Minotto, for nearly three decades, was his elder brother Ernesto, also on bandoneón. And another long-stayer was violinist Octavio Scaglione, who joined in 1926 and was still with Canaro thirty years later. Listen to:

  * *Loca* (1938) when Scaglione comes in at 1 minute 42 seconds.

Canaro's long-term bass player was Olindo Sinibaldi, who left him for D'Arienzo in 1940. Sinibaldi was also the chosen bass player for the Quintets Don Pancho/Pirincho, together with Riccardi (piano), Di Cicco (bandoneón), Scaglione and Gallastegui (violins). This was a clear indication that these were Canaro's favourites.

Surprisingly little or no credit is given to the musicians who provided the woodwind and brass. In his extensive autobiography Canaro makes no reference to them, but he does include photographs of his orchestras from the mid 1920s to 1940s, two of which show several members holding or playing trombone, clarinet and trumpet.

No one individual provided the distinctive tones of the clarinet and trumpet. However, we do know that in 1932 the trumpeter José Ranieri joined the orchestra and can be heard most distinctly in the ranchera recording *Las Margaritas* (1932) and in the rousing *Silencio* (1933) – and thereafter in numerous tangos, valses and milongas in to the 1940s.

Canaro Summary

- Prolific and enduring
- Beautiful tango, valses, and milongas
- Brass, woodwind, & organ
- Hard businessman with soft heart

Francisco Lomuto

Personal Story

Francisco Lomuto was born in 1893 in the Buenos Aires barrio, or neighbourhood, of Parque Patricios (forty-eight years later he recorded the well-known milonga *'Parque Patricios'*). His parents were immigrants from Italy, musicians who often played tangos at home. His father, Victor, was a guitarist, violinist and bandoneonist, while his mother Rosalía was a pianist. They had twelve children, three of whom died young, leaving three daughters and six sons. Four of the sons became musicians.

Francisco, the eldest boy, was taught piano by his mother and was clearly gifted. At the age of thirteen he composed his first tango named El 606, a reference to the medical treatment of syphilis! It was published and became so popular that in 1909 it was recorded by the Municipal Band of Buenos Aires. By this time, aged fifteen, Francisco was employed in a music store, playing sheet music to encourage sales.

Meanwhile back to his brothers. Victor learnt bandoneón and went to Paris to play with the successful Bianco-Bachicha orchestra. Enrique became a pianist, formed his own orquesta típica and recorded tangos – although he did not achieve any great commercial success. Héctor became a successful jazzman, set up his own band and performed regularly on radio. The two remaining brothers went in different directions, but even they influenced his tango. Oscar, a journalist, wrote the lyrics to Nunca Más (composed & recorded by Francisco), and Blas (a high ranking Naval officer who in the 1940s held prominent positions in the government of President Perón) helped to elevate his brother as the orchestra of choice to entertain the military establishment.

In about 1920 Francisco Lomuto became an apprentice of the already famous Francisco Canaro, having asked if he could join his orchestra in order to learn the trade of running his own. Generously Canaro agreed to take him on and in 1923 Lomuto directed his first orchestra (the one already assembled by his younger brother Enrique).

He joined the same record company as Canaro – Odeon. In 1926 and 1927 both were recording with their respective jazz bands. Lomuto continued with Odeon until 1931 when he moved to the Victor label, and changed his orchestra's name to Orquesta Típica Sinfonica.

As a result of Lomuto's early collaboration with Canaro there are many similarities with Canaro's music in the 1920s and 30s, and not only in overall structure and sound. They recorded many of the same tangos, often in the same years. For example, in March 1929 Canaro recorded an instrumental version of *Soy Un Arlequin*, then three months later Lomuto released *Soy Un Arlequin* with a singer – Canaro's singer, Charlo. This pattern continued for years, one of them first recording and releasing a tango to be followed some months later by the other one. We can see this as late as August 1938 when both orchestras recorded *Desaliento*. But these dual releases do not appear to have been done competitively as Francisco Canaro and Francisco Lomuto were friends and stayed friends. They were also jointly influential organisers of SADAIC, the organisation to protect copyright of tango music and lyrics.

Lomuto was a prolific tango composer. His work included *Nunca Más*, *Sombras Nada Mas* (recorded by Canaro two weeks after Lomuto's version) and *Candombe Criollo* (which Canaro recorded with even less of a time gap).

Francisco Lomuto was a big bear of a man, tall and stout and well liked, often described by those who met him as a gentleman, jovial, amiable. He was particularly remembered for his ever-present cigarette or cigar – a relentless smoker, he died aged fifty-seven.

Signature Sounds

The overall feel of Lomuto's music is simple and like Canaro's it is easy to listen to and easy to dance to. As with Canaro, he achieves this with a steady clear walking rhythm and simple melodies, but unlike Canaro his sound is not mellow. The recordings are harsher in the upper register, and his steady clear rhythm is heavier, resembling the footfall of an elephant. More than that, the bass line has a faster pace – like an elephant with somewhere really important to get to.

Listen to the difference in bass line and upper register between these two versions:
   * *Tormenta* (Lomuto 1939);
   * *Tormenta* (Canaro 1939).

Staying with the African animal analogies, most of Lomuto's danceable tangos have explosions in the upper register, creating a racing beat reminiscent of a stampede of gazelle across the grasslands. Listen to the stampeding gazelles above the heavy, hurrying elephants:
   * *La Gayola* (1941)

The two Franciscos were influenced by that other popular music of the time - jazz. As a result both often introduced woodwind instruments, in particular the clarinet. When we hear a clarinet in a tango, we should think 'Is it Canaro or Lomuto?' By listening for heavy elephant feet, and a stampede, you should be able to form a conclusion. But if you are still not sure then there are two other clear signature sounds that cry out 'Lomuto'.

The first comes from his love of the marching band – undoubtedly helped by the Municipal Band of Buenos Aires recording his first tango composition, and probably helped too by the marching bands of his patrons, the Argentine Navy. This signature sound is the clashing of cymbals.

Lomuto used cymbals in many of his commonly played late 1930s recordings, and so hearing one is an immediate and clear identifier of Lomuto. Cymbals do appear occasionally in other orchestra recordings – there is for example a discrete cymbal strike in the closing section (at 2 minutes 24 seconds) of Fresedo's *Buscándote*, and another in Caló's *Corazón No Lo Hagas Caso* – but there is nothing else about those tracks that could suggest Lomuto. Listen to:

   * *Madreselva* (1938)

The second signature sound used by Lomuto is his ending of a tango. He applies a diminished 7th chord, a sound that is often used in jazz. The traditional tango ending (used by Canaro for example) is called the 'chan chan' and has a 'down Up!' effect, chan-CHAN! Lomuto's ending however is more 'Up! down.', CHAN...chan, creating an effect that does not quite allow the listener to rest. Listen to:

* *La Melodía de Nuestro Adiós* (1938) and compare the ending with Canaro's. Then listen to a random selection of Lomuto endings from the 1930s onwards to become familiar with this unique ending.

Often with tango, if you cannot pin down the orchestra, it is worth waiting for the end!

Singers

Lomuto is mostly associated with two singers - Fernando Díaz and Jorge Omar.

Fernando Díaz recorded the most with Lomuto (one hundred and seventy tracks) from 1931 to early 1943, and was one of the most popular and best-paid singers of the day. Before he joined Lomuto he had sung with Di Sarli in his 1929 sextet, and a bit later with the Orquesta Típica Victor, Carabelli, and other now lesser-known orchestras. Díaz's voice is strong and fits well with Lomuto's throbbing, elephantine bass lines. You can hear him in *La Gayola* (1941).

The second star singer was Jorge Omar – real name Juan Manuel Ormaechea. Juan used to be in a duet with a guitarist called Jorge Omar, and after he broke away to perform on his own he used his guitarist friend's name. His first recording was in 1935 and he stayed eight years with Lomuto, making one hundred and thirty-six recordings. He can be seen singing alongside Lomuto in the film '*Melgarejo*'.

Díaz and Omar recorded duets together but most of them were other rhythms, with only one tango and a couple of vals and milongas.

Other singers that are worth a mention in the popular dance context include Canaro's star singer Charlo, who was mainly with Lomuto from 1928 to 1930. There are many great tracks but the surviving recording quality often means that they are not played at today's milongas. It is a sign of the closeness between them that Lomuto was able to share Canaro's singer. In 1928 alone Charlo recorded nearly two hundred tracks for Canaro and fifty for Lomuto – sometimes he sang for them on the same day. Charlo would remain in the Odeon studios whilst his accompanying orchestra changed.

Much later in the 1940s (towards the end of the orchestra's recording life) came singers such as Carlos Galarce, Alberto Rivera and Miguel Montero. They are all worth listening to as they bring a more serene feel to the Lomuto sound, but they are less frequently heard in today's milongas.

Musicians

Lomuto had regular woodwind, brass, and percussion musicians embedded in his orchestra. The lovely rich signature sounds of the clarinet belong to Carmelo Águila and Primo Staderi. We can attribute the cornet to Natalio Nappe and from 1938 the trumpet to Cándido Borrajo (who was on loan from his brother Héctor Lomuto's jazz band). The cymbals were manned by Desio Salvador Cilota, and as for the elephantine double bass player, that was the wonderfully named Hamlet Greco (who in 1945 joined the Di Sarli orchestra). These musicians also contributed to the occasional sounds of oboe, saxophone, drums, and cello.

Hamlet Greco was one of the very few bass players to be given the opportunity to play prominently. Listen to:
  * *Nostalgias* (1936) - from about 52 seconds.

The pianist from 1930 to 1942 (the period that we mostly hear at milongas today, with singers Jorge Omar and Fernando Díaz) was Oscar Napolitano. We can hear him play on every track, but Lomuto does not make a feature of the piano, and so in 1937 Oscar took the opportunity to give himself an opening solo on the keyboard with his own vals composition *Idolatria*. He was a talented, well-respected musician who worked with Lomuto for many years. When he married in 1939 he enjoyed the tribute of the Lomuto orchestra providing the music both at the ceremony and at the celebration afterwards.

During the main dance music years the regular bandoneonists were Martin Darré, Américo Figola and Luis Zinkes, while the violinists were Armando Guttierez and Leopoldo Schiffrin.

Lomuto Summary

- Apprentice to Canaro
- Jovial, stout, heavy smoker
- Woodwind and cymbals
- Unique ending, CHAN...chan

Edgardo Donato

Personal Story

Edgardo Donato established his tango credentials in Montevideo, Uruguay, but he was born in Buenos Aires in 1897. His parents were Italian immigrants and musicians and they moved their family across the Río de la Plata to Montevideo whilst Edgardo was a young boy.

Edgardo, like two of his brothers, was sent to music school, and he learnt the full range of musical styles from classical, opera, through to the new jazz – but he had his own strong and particular musical personality from the earliest days. One of his teachers was infuriated by Edgardo's irrepressible habit of playing games with his violin, such as plucking the strings in the most inappropriate pieces. Francisco Canaro remembers seeing him on stage in the mid 1920s plucking his violin, playing it behind his head and even throwing it up in the air and catching it without losing the beat. Donato it seems was a tango punk!

In 1927 Edgardo teamed up with the Uruguayan violinist Roberto Zerillo, who had already played in Argentina for Osvaldo Fresedo, and they formed their own orchestra 'Donato-Zerillo'. It was soon spotted and hired by a tango impresario to play in Buenos Aires – which they did from 1928 to 1930. Things were looking great for the Donato-Zerillo orchestra - regular prestigious performances, radio broadcasts, recording contracts. They even had the superstar singer Azucena Maizani performing with them. Then Maizani and Zerillo became romantically involved, and Zerillo went off with her to tour Europe.

Donato set up his own orchestra, Edgardo Donato Y Sus Muchachos, supported by his brothers Osvaldo and Ascanio on piano and cello respectively, and soon developed the freer more playful style that defines him. He can be seen directing this orchestra in 1933 in the film *'Tango!'*.

As we will see later, Donato had a successful and happy time until his orchestra unravelled in the early 1940s due to sackings, resignations, and poaching by his pianist brother Osvaldo. He continued recording until 1961, but the sparkle and the dance rhythms had gone.

Donato was a prolific composer of tangos. One of the earliest was the now omnipresent *A Media Luz*, famously scribbled down on a streetcar ride across Montevideo. Amongst his other greatest hits were *Se Va La Vida*; *El Huracán* (also recorded by D'Arienzo & De Angelis); *T.B.C* (recorded by Di Sarli); and *El Acomodo* (also recorded by Canaro).

Signature Sounds

The overall feel of Donato's music is upbeat and fun. His rhythms are choppy and high energy for the dancer, and in some ways he should be credited as the forerunner of the D'Arienzo revolution in 1936 (although this is one of tango's many hot debates). Listen to:

 * *El Acomodo* (1933)

You can also hear the low violin that was to become part of D'Arienzo's signature sound.

Donato makes great use of the violin pizzicato style – not picking with a single finger in the European style but strumming several fingers over the strings like a guitar, – which sometimes sounds like a banjo. He was not the creator of this sound (it is rooted in the Afro-Río de la Plata influence of using stringed instruments percussively) but he was a popular adopter. Listen to:

 * *Tierrita* (1934)

There is something in Donato's music that is very different to other orchestras. The tone of his music is somehow brighter. This is due to a particular instrument amongst the bandoneón line up - the piano accordion. Donato introduced this innovation in 1934, by which time he was already a huge success, having recorded hundreds of tangos, regularly performing on radio and appearing in the 1933 film *'Tango!'*. So this instrument was an experiment and one that helped define him anew.

The accordion sound is evocative of a Parisian street musician, and once your ear becomes attuned to it you will be surprised by how many times it appears in Donato's tangos, valses, and milongas, mainly lifting the bandoneón section. After 1938, the accordion increasingly started to feature in short solo bursts. Listen to:

   * *Alas Rotas* (1938)

However, in a way Canaro beat him to it. Whilst Donato's recordings in 1935 include the accordion, he does not use it in full Parisian style, which is where Canaro steps in to record *No Nos Veremos Más* (1935). The listener is taken aback when the accordion starts up, played by lead bandoneonist Minotto Di Cicco. But we do not hear much more of that experiment from Canaro, hence the sound is now associated only with Donato.

Another signature sound of Donato is the unusual showcasing of a female singer, particularly in duet.

Singers

Donato was an innovator, not only in his composition of now classic tangos, nor in the early introduction of high-energy rhythmic tangos, nor in the unexpected introduction of the piano accordion. He also dared to bring in a female singer to front a dance orchestra. Why is this a surprising move, given that there were many famous female tango singers? The female tango singers were hugely successful as soloists in cabaret, theatre, film, radio and records, but it was rare for them to perform for a dance audience.

Lita Morales features from 1937 to 1941, often in duet with Horacio Lagos or Romeo Gavioli, but frequently given the lead. Listen to:
   * *Carnaval de Mi Barrio* (1939)

Horacio Lagos recorded over sixty tango, vals and milongas (comprising the majority of Donato's vocal tracks that we dance to today), whether solo or in duet with Lita Morales or Romeo Gavioli. Listen to:
   * *El Adiós* (1938)

Romeo Gavioli, a Uruguayan, was a singer, violinist, composer and bandleader, and one of the first people to promote the musical form of candombe in to the repertoire of tango orquestas típicas. Listen to his voice in:

Mendocina (1942)

The recordings of the singers are in all permutations: Lagos alone, Morales alone, Gavioli alone, Lagos and Morales, Gavioli and Morales, and Lagos and Gavioli. The songs they sing are upbeat and fun-filled, a mood often reflected in the faces of the happy dancers who are often blissfully unaware of the drama, tension, passion, and heartbreak that was being played out behind the scenes in the studio. The singers were paired up not just in songs but also in their private lives.

Horacio Lagos and Lita Morales were married and already recording with Donato when in 1939 Donato recruited Romeo Gavioli, inadvertently introducing a real Romeo in to the marriage. Romeo and Lita became 'romantically involved', creating a turbulent love triangle, and Donato found himself struggling to manage, console, and command his star performers.

Lita's last recording for Donato was in February 1941, while apparently pregnant, and she did not return to a recording studio until 1955. The two love rivals continued recording (under Donato's controlled conditions) until 6th August 1942, when both recorded the duet *Lonjazos*. Whatever happened on that day in the studio is unclear, but it was the last time that either of them recorded for Donato. Shortly afterwards the entire orchestra of Donato y Sus Muchachos disintegrated.

Horacio Lagos is known to have sung next in 1943 with a breakaway orchestra led by Edgardo's brother Osvaldo. Romeo Gavioli continued on his own in 1943 and 1944, recording mainly candombes, and went on to do some theatre work.

In 1957 Romeo, having fallen into decline, committed suicide by driving off a pier in to the Río de la Plata aged only forty-four. It is not known whether his sad end was linked to those intense days of some fifteen years earlier, nor what became of Horacio and Lita's marriage.

Prior to the tragic trio, the other singers Donato employed included Luis Díaz (from Orquestas Típicas Victor, Los Provincianos, and Brunswick); Teófilo Ibáñez (Orquestas Típicas Victor, Porteña, Brunswick and the sextets of Fresedo & Firpo); Félix Guttierez (briefly with Francisco Canaro); and Antonio Maida (the younger brother of Canaro's star singer Roberto Maida).

And finally, for those of you who study the printed record labels, you may have seen the mysteriously named Randona as a Donato duet singer. This is the alternative name for his violinist, Armando Julio Piovani, who from time to time stepped up to the microphone. Listen to:

   * *Sacale Punta* (1938).

Musicians

Who were the violinists responsible for those pizzicatos that characterise Donato's music? In the main, Edgardo Donato himself, of course. His character is in those strings, even when conducting the other violinists, such as his long time colleague Armando Julio Piovani.

The signature sound of the piano accordion is produced by Osvaldo Bertone, known as Bertolin, who was only thirteen years old when he joined Edgardo's orchestra in 1934. Despite his youth he was already an experienced player and performer. He had learnt to play aged four, and by six he was playing publicly in a cinema providing the music for silent films.

Bertolin is ever present in Donato's tangos, valses, and milongas until his last day with Donato (6th August 1942), when he recorded *Mendocina*, a vals in which his piano accordion is featured out in front.

Edgardo Donato's pianist is his brother Osvaldo who composed many of the orchestra's popular recordings such as *Sacale Punta*, *Un Libro*, and jointly with Edgardo *El Huracán*. He can be heard in all of Donato's recordings from 1932 to 1942. Osvaldo formed his own orchestra in 1943, taking many of Edgardo's musicians with him and recruiting the recently departed singer Horacio Lagos.

Edgardo's other brother, cellist Ascanio, is similarly on all of the recordings from 1932 to 1942, but is a little harder to pick out.

The bandoneonists were Miguel Bonano (whose earlier European tour included performances before the King of Spain and, separately, Benito Mussolini), Juan Turturiello and Vicente Vilardi. Their combined throbbing contribution keeps the dancers on the move.

Donato Summary

- Round-rimmed glasses
- Tango punk violinist
- Parisian-sound accordion
- Love triangle singers

Orquesta Típica Victor

Personal Story

The Orquesta Típica Victor story is different to the other nineteen orchestras – it did not perform in public; it is not identified by its orchestra leader; and it did not have permanent members, only using musicians who were available when it was time to record.

It reminds me of Dr Frankenstein's monster – constructed from the parts of different bodies, but ultimately developing its own personality. It was a success in the laboratory, or recording studio, but the creators did not allow it to go out in public. I am sure that it is a coincidence that Dr Frankenstein's first name was 'Victor'!

Let me deal with the name, Orquesta Típica Victor. All of the twenty orchestras, except that of Rodríguez, were in fact 'orquestas típicas'. The term means that they played predominantly tangos in a particular style. The original longer description explains what that style was - 'orquesta típica criolla', a creole or home-grown style, as opposed to European or North American. The term dates back to about 1911 in Buenos Aires and a tango recording by bandoneonist Vicente Greco, who is credited with coming up with it, but it is more likely to have been created by the record company who needed to label and market the new sound. In his memoires, Francisco Canaro claims all of the credit for devising the name. The 'Victor' part of the name comes from the company Victor Records, also known for a while as the Victor Talking Machine Company.

The Orquesta Típica Victor, now generally known as OTV, recorded from 1925 to 1944. We tend to hear only a small percentage of their output because the majority suffers from poor sound quality reproductions. Despite being an 'Orquesta Típica', it made over one hundred non-tango records – including foxtrots, polkas, rancheras, corridos, pasodobles, marchas, boleros, rumbas, and zambas – amounting to nearly a quarter of its total output. Today many tango aficionados of the 'Golden Age' can be quite dismissive of other musical forms, whereas their hero–maestros such as Canaro, Lomuto, Donato, Firpo, and D'Arienzo frequently varied their portfolios to include other rhythms.

Evidence concerning the leadership of OTV in the early days is scarce and often contradictory, probably reflecting the commercial scramble to establish the experimental in-house orchestra. The idea began in the United States of America, which was the home of the Victor Talking Machine Company, however the OTV that we recognise today came only after Victor had established a recording facility in Buenos Aires. The first recording was made in November 1925. As for the hidden face of OTV, the orchestra leader, there were several, and there were none...

A number of authoritative books and articles credit Luis Petrucelli as being the orchestra leader from November 1925 right through to 1931, and Adolfo Carabelli taking up the reins from 1932 to 1935. But it would be more accurate to say that the formation of OTV as a recording tour de force was due to Victor's artistic director Adolfo Carabelli (who was a virtuoso jazz musician without any tango experience). Carabelli called on the tanguero Luis Petrucelli to form the orquesta típica and to choose the material, but neither Petrucelli nor Carabelli were designated, nor acted as, sole orchestra leader. Petrucelli, for example, only months after helping to set up OTV, was in New York playing with Francisco Canaro - dressed up in gaucho-esque costume. On his return to Buenos Aires he formed his own sextet and recorded with it until 1931. When he was available he went in to the Victor studios to contribute to recordings, but he was an influential session musician for OTV, rather than the orchestra leader, in its strictest sense.

Carabelli was more prominent than Petrucelli. His role was not only to bear the corporate responsibility to succeed, but also to contribute his classically trained musical talent and his experience of leading a successful jazz orchestra. From 1931 he was, in the main, also the OTV pianist.

To add an extra level of fluidity to the whole arrangement, Victor released recordings (by more or less the same musicians) under the name Orquesta Típica Porteña from January 1930 to August 1931, and under the name Orquesta Típica Los Provincianos from 1931 to 1934. The core membership of the former was Carabelli (piano), Petrucelli and Ortiz (bandoneón), and Vardaro (violin). The latter formation was led by Ciriaco Ortiz, who had alongside him the bandoneonist Aníbal Troilo.

Just as Petrucelli pursued his separate career outside of OTV, so too did Carabelli, who recorded under his own name from September 1931 to July 1934. His orquesta típica, like OTV, did not perform live and his musicians were mainly the same as those recording as OTV.

The last recording for OTV under Carabelli's stewardship was in February 1935. Then there was a gap of fourteen months until the next recording under the musical direction of Federico Scorticati, who took the role from February 1936 to November 1941. Scorticati had been a bandoneonist with Carabelli and OTV since 1931, and had clearly impressed the Victor executives who were looking for a post-Carabelli leader. Nevertheless he was a surprise choice to lead what was by then a high profile orchestra.

The reasoning was that his tango musical roots and playing experience were exceptional. His curriculum vitae included being orchestra leader on radio shows such as the prestigious Radio Belgrano, and earlier in his career he had played in high quality orchestras such as Canaro and Di Sarli. In contrast, his own estimation of his suitability for the role was less confident. In a later interview, he said that he found those radio orchestra experiences extremely difficult because he was neither a natural leader of musicians nor a businessman - in fact he simply says that he 'was not made to be an orchestra leader'!

However, the Victor executives knew what they were doing. OTV continued to be successful under Federico Scorticati's stewardship despite his self-doubt, and they recorded over ninety tracks, with about half of them being non-tango numbers.

After Scorticati's departure in November 1941 there were no further recordings for nearly two years. Pianist and arranger Mario Maurano took over in September 1943 and recorded until May 1944, a period that included many hits still frequently played today in milongas around the world. Like Carabelli and Petrucelli before him, Maurano continued to lead and record with his own orchestra at the same time as stewarding OTV recording sessions.

Signature Sounds

Just because OTV is in Part One of the book, 'The Simple', it does not mean that the orchestra maintained a limited style over the course of nineteen years and over four hundred recordings. There are 'rhythmic' and 'lyrical' tangos in their repertoire too, but to me the overall feel of their music fits into 'The Simple'.

The OTV style uses relatively simple constructions with limited counter melody lines, without complex changes of speed but with the common techniques include pizzicato and low, fourth string violin expressions.

OTV does have its own sound but it does not have any particular *signature* sounds. The overall sound and feel of the music is identifiably 'OTV', but there is no particular instrument, nor a particular musician's style of playing, which stands out as uniquely OTV.

We can hear the passing of the decades and the orchestra leaders from a sample recording from each of the four periods when we listen to:
* *El Chamuyo* (1930), the Petrucelli era;
* *Jueves* (1934), the Carabelli era;
* *Adiós Buenos Aires (1938),* the Scorticati era;
* *Bajo El Cono Azul* (1944) the Maurano era.

Sometimes the best way to identify an orchestra is by way of elimination. Is the music simple? Are there any revealing instruments such as trumpet (Canaro), cymbals (Lomuto), accordion (Donato)? Is an instrument taking a clear lead, like the piano (Firpo)? Is it choppy in short sharp staccato bursts, with phrases punctuated by piano (D'Arienzo, Biagi)? Do the endings have revealing features (Tanturi/Rodríguez)? If none of the signature sounds of other orchestras is present, it is likely to be OTV. Listen to:

* *El Chamuyo* (1930)

As OTV moves in to the late 1930s to mid 1940s the music, following the general trend, becomes more lyrical, and so we need to ask different questions to differentiate from other lyrical orchestras. Is there a harp or vibraphone (Fresedo)? Is there a constant piano keeping the rhythm and bridging the phrases (Di Sarli)? Is there a signature ending (Caló)? Are there soaring violins (De Angelis)? Is there an alternation between lyrical and rhythmic phrases, with a changing of lead instrument (D'Agostino/Demare)? If none of these signature sounds is present either, it is likely to be OTV. Listen to:

* *Adiós Buenos Aires* (1938)

The singer is Angel Vargas. As soon as he starts singing, we think of the orchestra of Angel D'Agostino. The structure of the track is very similar to the (future) signature 'Call and Response' structure of D'Agostino with the switching of lead instrument. And yet this is an

Simple: OTV

OTV track. Sometimes DJs play this in a tanda with D'Agostino/Vargas, because it can fit better there than with other OTV tracks.

We have to accept that identifying tango tracks is not always as straightforward as we would like! Getting to know tango music is not an exact science, and often comes down to emotional recognition.

Singers

On the 8th October 1928, after recording one hundred and thirty-three instrumentals, the combined mind of OTV decided that the violinist Antonio Buglione should step up to the microphone and sing. Buglione was not a reckless gamble, since he had been singing for a couple of years with many orchestras (including Canaro, Lomuto, Fresedo), but he had not previously been mentioned on the record credits. Listen to:

* *Hembra* (1928)

Buglione was the composer of *La Maleva*, a tango often heard at today's milongas, which was recorded by Biagi, Caló, Canaro, Troilo and D'Arienzo.

From as early as 1922 Roberto Díaz had been with the Victor company recording non-tango tracks, and in December 1928 he moves in to OTV becoming the regular singer until 1931, at the same time singing with the associated formations of Orquestas Típicas Porteña and Los Provincianos. Listen to:

* *Vieja Calesita* (1929)

Díaz has a place in tango history. Francisco Canaro credits him with being the first *estribillista* (the singer of the chorus) when he recorded with Canaro in 1926.

In October 1929 Ernesto Famá joined the guest singers and by 1930 the field began opening up to better-known singers, among them many household names. Over the nineteen-year life of the orchestra there were twenty-five singers, although not all of them sang tango as OTV had a sizeable repertoire of other rhythms. Amongst them are names known to us from other well known orchestras: Angel Vargas (D'Agostino); Francisco Fiorentino (Troilo); Fernando Díaz (Lomuto); Lita Morales (Donato); Charlo (Canaro and Lomuto); Famá (Canaro); Ibáñez (Biagi); Corrales, later known as Pomar (Di Sarli); and Alberto Gómez (Carabelli, OTs Provincianos & Porteña, Donato) – although on the OTV labels Gómez is known as 'Nico', one of several of his alternative names.

With such diversity, it is clearly not possible to use the singer's characteristics as a point of identification of the orchestra.

Musicians

We know many of the musicians who at some point recorded with OTV, but because the line up was so fluid, using available musicians otherwise contracted to other orchestras, we can not be completely sure about who is playing on which particular track.

Some of the more well known, well-respected (often revered) musicians included bandoneonists-turned-orchestra-leaders: Luis Petrucelli (original OTV front man, who died in 1941 aged only thirty-eight); the young Aníbal Troilo; Pedro Laurenz; Carlos Marcucci; Ciriaco Ortiz; and the later OTV front man Federico Scorticato.

Amongst the violinists were the musicians' musicians Cayetano Puglisi (later the long serving violinist for Juan D'Arienzo); Elvino Vardaro (another legend closely linked to Troilo, Pugliese, Fresedo, and Di Sarli); and Agesilao Ferrazzano.

The notable pianists were the OTV leaders Adolfo Carabelli from 1932 to 1935, and Mario Maurano from September 1943 to May 1944.

OTV Summary

- Assembly of changing session artists
- No public performances
- Four different 'leaders'

Roberto Firpo

Personal Story

Roberto Firpo was born in the Greater Province of Buenos Aires in 1884 and, as an impoverished fourteen year old, he ventured into the city to earn a living, at anything. As an unskilled labourer he went from one low-paid job to another, including painting the doors and window frames of the newly built Congressional Palace. In about 1904, when working in a steel factory, he met Juan Deamboggio (later known as Bachicha, who came to tango fame in Paris with Eduardo Bianco). Those were the days when Firpo was entertaining himself with a homemade xylophone consisting of an array of partly filled glass bottles, while dreaming of playing the piano. Deamboggio was learning bandoneon and introduced Firpo to his teacher, the tango composer Alfredo Bevilacqua (a family friend of the D'Agostinos).

Firpo had come to music relatively late in life, in as much as he was having piano lessons aged twenty, but at a time when tango was still young. And, fortunately for the development of tango, his path thereafter brought him into contact with the most influential of the tango pioneers, with whom he socialised and from whom he learnt. He soon became a force for change and innovation in the genre, which up to that point had consisted of solo performers – usually with no musical training and, more often than not, leading a dissolute lifestyle.

By 1912 he had introduced the piano to tango recordings and by his early thirties, in 1917 and 1918, he was directing a substantial tango orchestra from his piano stool. It included Eduardo Arolas, Osvaldo Fresedo and Bachicha on bandoneón, whilst his violinists included Francisco Canaro, Cayetano Puglisi, and Ferrazzano. He had the most innovative and influential bass player of the day, the Afro-Argentinian Leopoldo Thompson, and he was an early adopter of the clarinet (played by Juan Carlos Bazan).

Firpo soon became not just the personification of tango but its ringmaster. He began to control everything, frequently to the detriment of young start-ups. Even the pugnacious Canaro had difficulty breaking through Firpo's tenacious hold on recording and performing monopolies.

Despite the magnitude of Firpo's presence in the music and business of the tango world during the 1910s and 1920s, his legacy is not heard frequently at twenty-first century milongas. The majority of his tangos (of which there were an extraordinary one thousand five hundred) were acoustic recordings (or the earliest electric recordings) and their poor technical quality does not lend itself to easy listening for dancing. This scarcity is further aggravated by today's record companies failing to release his material. The few good quality and danceable tracks that are available from that early period are during the years 1927 to 1929, a decade after his peak dominance.

Tango history books all report that Firpo retired from the music business in 1930. It is an interesting thought that one of the most prolific tango greats retired after decades of active service at a time when many of the most popular maestros had not even started.

Firpo's own account of this episode is that, as a self-made millionaire, he envisaged himself as a great landowner and so he invested everything he had into a sizeable ranch. To cut a long and painful story very short, that adventure did not work out for him and he lost most of his fortune, forcing him to return to tango. However, a look at his uninterrupted recording history does not support this idea of a retirement and a return to work. It is possible that retirement for Firpo meant stopping or reducing his public and radio performances because he clearly still managed to visit the Buenos Aires studios to maintain a healthy recording output.

Undeterred by losing most of his long and hard-earned fortune, he once again became prolific, innovative, and commercially successful – both with his quintet recordings from 1936 and those of his fuller symphonic orchestra.

Firpo's legacy also included his extensive catalogue of compositions that includes *Alma de Bohemio*, *El Amanecer*, *Vea Vea*, and *Fuegos Artificiales.*

Just as many evenings of tango social dancing end with the playing of *La Cumparsita,* let us end this section with Firpo's contribution to that most famous of tango songs. His own recorded versions are not often heard, nor did he compose it, nor did he make it universally popular, but he 'discovered' it and 'tangofied' it. One day in February 1916 in a Montevideo cafe, La Giralda, he was given a partly composed marching tune that had the potential for a tango rhythm. He merged some of his own discarded material with it (written as far back as 1906) and played the new creation one night at that same cafe. The customers loved it. In November 1916 he recorded it in Buenos Aires, and over the next two years it was recorded by several others, including Juan Maglio and Osvaldo Fresedo. But then it disappeared, forgotten, until 1924 when the lyrics *Si Superieras* (written for a stage song yet to be composed) were put together with the tune of *La Cumparsita* and it became successful – so successful that Carlos Gardel recorded it and then, of course, everybody else did for many decades to come.

Signature Sounds

From the perspective of the twenty-first century milonga-goer it is difficult to appreciate the overwhelming success and dominance of Roberto Firpo's music in the 1910s, 20s and 30s. But why was he so successful at that time, and why is he not so popular now?

He was in many ways what modern business terminology calls a 'First Mover'. He benefited from being the first (or the strongest amongst the firsts) to enter the booming tango industry. The advantage of this good timing gave him the opportunity to build superior brand recognition that led to early customer (or fan) loyalty, and to negotiate commercial exclusivity or preferential deals in publicity, recording and performing rights. In all of these areas Firpo applied himself assertively.

He was a tango pioneer and innovator, but his defining sound and style came prior to the availability of good quality recording technology. That defining signature sound was the piano, whose power replaced the role of the guitar in early tango, providing the rhythm, the melody, and the bridge between phrases. By the time the recording technology had progressed enough for us to appreciate him (in what we now consider to be the extremely early years of 1927/29), there is no longer an element of novelty to differentiate between his sound and those of his peers such as Canaro, Lomuto, and OTV. However, listen to:

* *Pablo* (1927)

Pablo has the familiar slow tempo of the era, the pizzicato and the low, slow violin but the piano is present throughout. The other orchestras of the time have the piano as a standard instrument (thanks to Firpo) but it is not always so prominent.

By the late 1920s there were signs that the tango genre was at risk of losing popularity. There was little that was new or exciting for the public who were being tempted by new crazes such as jazz. Firpo responded in the early 1930s by increasing the number of non-tango recordings such as polka, foxtrot, pasodoble, and rancheras. Then from the mid-1930s he responded to the emerging tango symphonic style (made popular by De Caro, Fresedo, Canaro). Listen to:

* *Desconsuelo* (1936);

* *No Quiero Verte Llorar* (1937).

In 1936, as well as continuing with his orchestra, he formed a quintet, '*Los de Antes*' (meaning 'Those from days gone by'). The idea behind forming the quintet was twofold. Firstly to counter the larger symphonic orchestras with a much simpler sound predicated on, but not copying, the 'Old Guard' style. And secondly, to speed up the music to match the recently emerged dance energy of D'Arienzo. Canaro said that Firpo's quintet was indeed one hundred per cent authentic creole tango in its rhythm, melody, and beat. Listen to the wonderfully cheerful:

* *La Trilla* (1936);
* *El Moro* (1937).

Despite the improved recording quality of the quintet tracks, and their success when released in the mid to late 1930s, today they tend to be played mainly as 'specials' to lift the mood, particularly the milongas and valses which are fast and light-hearted. Listen to:

* the vals *Artedecer Campero* (1936)
* the milonga *El Esquinazo* (1939)

The Singers

As great as Firpo was in terms of tango creativity and industry, he is not associated with any outstanding singers.

Although his extensive discography is overwhelmingly instrumental there are a few interesting singers. The inevitable Old Guard-style stars Teófilo Ibáñez and Luis Díaz put in early appearances, as did the endearingly named Blue Prince (Principe Azul), who, as a cabaret compere, bestowed the title 'King of the Beat' upon Juan D'Arienzo. Carlos Varela recorded about seventy tracks in the mid 1930s (although such was Firpo's output that this was still only a small part of his discography). Varela's recording of *Cero A Cero* (1935) became a massive hit, helped by being the weekly anthem sung by thousands at Argentina's football stadia.

The Musicians

The piano is the obvious centre of Firpo's music and it is he at the keyboard in the recordings, although at times during live performances he would grandstand as the conductor waving the baton whilst others, such as Luis Cosenza, played the piano.

Whenever a clarinet can be heard in Firpo's recordings before 1935 then it is Juan Carlos Bazan (who can be seen playing in the 1933 film *'Tango!'*).

In 1933 the sixteen-year old 'Wizard of the Bandoneón' Juan Cambareri joined Firpo, and can be heard in the quintet recordings playing with great energy and speed. Cambareri went on to successfully lead his own orchestra from 1948, retaining the fast bandoneón-fuelled style of Firpo's quintet.

Firpo Summary

- Oldest in this book
- Prolific pioneer but now little heard
- Brought us La Cumparsita

PART TWO:
THE RHYTHMIC

Juan D'Arienzo

Personal Story

Most tango histories have us believe that Juan D'Arienzo mysteriously burst on to the scene in 1935 with his revolutionary rhythmic sound, but of course there is a fuller, longer personal story.

D'Arienzo was born in 1900 to a middle-class family living in central Buenos Aires. He was the eldest of three, all of whom became musicians. His brother Ernani was a pianist and drummer, while his sister Josefina was a virtuoso pianist and singer. Juan himself studied music and showed an early talent for the violin – so much so that he was being paid to perform at the Zoological Gardens in Palermo aged only eleven years old. He was accompanied on piano by another future tango great, Angelito D'Agostino, also aged eleven, with whom he remained friends.

D'Arienzo's musical career followed the familiar path of playing in cinemas during the era of silent films, and then performing with various jazz bands until the mid 1920s, when he started to become involved in the tango scene. He played in various tango formations that included Angel D'Agostino on piano and the already legendary bandoneonist and composer Anselmo Aieta. It was in that period that he jointly formed the D'Arienzo-Visca sextet, but pianist Luis Visca left due to his father's death, leaving D'Arienzo to head the group in 1927. In 1928 D'Arienzo's uncle gave him the opportunity to make records. It was D'Arienzo's good fortune that his uncle was Alfredo Amendola, the founder of Atlanta Records in Argentina. However, the resulting recordings were not in any way remarkable and do not provide any clues about the D'Arienzo that was to emerge seven years later.

There were no further recordings by D'Arienzo at that time but he continued to perform, notably at the prestigious Chantecler cabaret where he built a significant following and attracted the attention of the tango movers and shakers. His impact was so significant that he was offered a role in the ground-breaking first 'talkie' film in Argentina – appropriately entitled *'Tango!'* (1933). He can be seen at the Chantecler, playing violin and leading his orchestra in his own composition *Chirusa*.

As a result of his ever-increasing popularity at the Chantecler and on radio, D'Arienzo began recording again in July 1935. The new sound he developed from the end of 1935 created a revolution on the contemporary tango scene – and like all revolutions, it created a rift between those who were for him and those who were against.

The new style contrasted with the sophisticated, refined sound of the early 1930s, which had evolved in order to appeal to the more discerning audiences outside of the bars, cafes and milongas. Osvaldo Fresedo (appearing in Part Three) was the personification of 'refined'; listen to his 1935 *Isla de Capri,* for example. As for the brothers Julio and Francisco De Caro (appearing in Part Four), they had elevated tango to almost classical complexity, as can be heard in the 1932 *La Casita de Mis Viejos.* Even the simpler Canaro was producing soft, symphonic sounds for the cabaret and theatre audiences; listen to the 1935 recording *Casas Viejas* from the theatre production '*Rascacielos*' of the same year.

What was D'Arienzo's new style? Well, he is said to have brought tango down from the ears to the feet, which to many aficionados was like dragging homo sapiens back to the Neanderthal era. But by doing so he created a new raw energy, drawing in an adoring young fan base and with it an explosion in demand for dance tango and the venues to go with it. Years later, when Troilo's orchestra members were listening to a radio broadcast of D'Arienzo and mocking the rapid sound, Aníbal Troilo admonished them, telling them that if it were not for D'Arienzo creating the demand for tango then none of the tango orchestras would be working.

Juan D'Arienzo, crowned 'King of the Beat', conducted his orchestra not only from centre stage but from all of the stage – as the years went by he became more and more theatrical, his gestures ranging from energetic passion to contrived clowning. Despite the stage play he was strict with his musicians, demanding total discipline in the combined sound - everything had to be delivered with the dancer in mind.

D'Arienzo composed about twenty tangos, plus another twenty in conjunction with others, mainly his pianist Fulvio Salamanca and/or his bandoneonist Héctor Varela. The compositions that are amongst those still most frequently played at today's milongas are *Paciencia* and *Nada Más* (also recorded by Francisco Canaro) and *Ya Lo Ves* (also recorded by Biagi).

Signature Sounds

The overall feel of D'Arienzo's music post 1935 is dominated by a clear staccato or choppy beat – a rhythm to dance to. In a 1949 interview, he said that his tango is above all rhythm and energy, and that the base of his orchestra was the piano. To that I can add that the pistons in his engine were the bandoneóns. Not only do they thump out the double-time steps to leave the dancers in no doubt about the beat, but they also use decorations to drive the dancers to a frenzy, particularly in the closing phrases.

However, we should be careful neither to oversimplify the D'Arienzo sound nor to overlook the significant changes in his orchestra formations and their associated sound.

We can study a potted history of the changing D'Arienzo orchestras, their style and sound over thirty years by listening to four of his versions of *Chirusa*:
* his first recording in 1928 gives us the familiar Old Guard style of the period. D'Arienzo is unremarkable amongst his peers;
* then notice how his 1933 film version is faster, in a more staccato style, but not yet with the sharp edge of the 1936/37 sound that we most associate now with D'Arienzo. It is because Biagi had not yet joined the orchestra;

* then listen to the 1940 version. The orchestra has a fuller, deeper energy pumped up by Fulvio Salamanca on piano and the lead violinist Cayetano Puglisi;
* and finally culminating in the 1958 big band sound that is still danceable but is beyond the main dance period.

For the purposes of this comparison of changing styles it is a great shame that he did not record *Chirusa* during the key 1935 to 1939 period, but you can listen to any of his tango recordings during this period to hear the distinctive sound.

From 1935 to the 1960s there are two distinct instruments that allow us to identify D'Arienzo: the piano and the violin.

Punctuating the choppy phrases are short, sharp high-end piano notes. This primary signature sound remained over the decades, even though the pianists changed. It defines D'Arienzo but it did not come from him - the originator was Rodolfo Biagi (more about him later).

The other defining signature sound is the 'buzzing bee'. In nearly every tango, vals and milonga recorded by D'Arienzo you will hear the distinctive drone of the bass string of the lead violin. The sound is soulful, almost mournful – not words generally associated with the music of D'Arienzo.

This violin technique is not D'Arienzo's. It belongs to a long established Old Guard style that can be heard in recordings by other orchestras such as Orquesta Típica Victor, but never (or hardly ever) alongside a staccato choppy style. The main exception is to be heard in Biagi's 1942 *Bélgica* when (at 1 minute 18 seconds) the 'buzzing bee' appears over an extremely staccato rhythm with Biagi striking the piano keys. The fourth string violin here is a clear and deliberate reference to D'Arienzo, but whether it is inserted as a mark of respect or to irritate him is not known!

For examples of D'Arienzo's use of these signature sounds, listen to almost any of his recordings!

* *El Flete* (1936);
* *La Morocha* (1937);
* *Dime Mi Amor* (1941);
* *Don Juan* (1950).

Singers

D'Arienzo was not a fan of tango singers. He was uncomfortable with them being seen as the stars of the tango orchestra, saying that the star was the beat not the singer. I suspect it is more accurate to say that he considered himself to be the star and did not want anybody else to take the limelight. One of the clues behind this suspicion is the way that he dismissed his pianist Rodolfo Biagi, who had been receiving ever-growing applause and appreciation, detracting from admiration for D'Arienzo himself. "There's only room for one star in this orchestra," the leader allegedly said.

D'Arienzo's stage antics (viewable in TV recordings as late as the 1960s) reveal his need to be the centre of attention. Watch the YouTube clips of him muscling in on the singer's moment, particularly when poor Osvaldo Ramos is singing *Remembranza* (1964). Alberto Podestá tells the story of how the singers used to dislike this posturing, particularly the way D'Arienzo directed them with his finger close to their faces. During one television show Mario Bustos, having warned D'Arienzo several times, finally bit the wagging finger!

From 1935 to 1937 D'Arienzo made fifty-eight recordings and all except five were instrumentals. Four of the tracks with lyrics were recorded with Walter Cabral and one with Enrique Carbel – both youngsters who went on to pursue singing careers outside of our twenty tango orchestras. Carbel's career was cut tragically short when he died suddenly aged only twenty-eight.

From 1938 to 1939 D'Arienzo admitted a singer to half of his recordings – Alberto Echagüe - formerly the singer of Angel D'Agostino who had recommended him to his old friend D'Arienzo.

Despite D'Arienzo's reticence to feature the human voice, the D'Arienzo/Echagüe combination worked well and is heard at practically every milonga. Echagüe's appeal to D'Arienzo was that he was not too artistic, did not take control of the tune and was a functional singer who delivered the lyrics on the beat – precisely what D'Arienzo (and his dancing fans) wanted. Listen to:
  * *El Flete* (1936)

In 1940 Echagüe was part of the mass exodus from D'Arienzo's orchestra (see the Musicians section below) and so over the next few years D'Arienzo recorded first with Alberto Reynal and later with Juan Carlos Lamas, but both were overshadowed in style by Vicente José Falivene. D'Arienzo, in tribute to his lead violinist and arranger Héctor Varela and his wife's maiden name (Mauré), gave Falivene the stage name Héctor Mauré. His first recording was in December 1940, and he continued until July 1944, leaving some fifty recordings. His contribution was that he changed the sound of

D'Arienzo. His voice was more than the beat. He sang with emotion and slowed D'Arienzo down. He was the voice of D'Arienzo's 1940s. Listen to:

   * *Dime Mi Amor* (1941)

In the summer of 1944 D'Arienzo convinced Echagüe to come back, and in six months Echagüe recorded twelve tracks (surprisingly, half of them were milongas). For the dancer in twenty-first century milongas this comeback does not work so well as there is neither the sharp staccato dance tango of 1938/39 nor the emotional depth of Mauré's voice. D'Arienzo was no longer an innovator – he had lost that position to Troilo, Di Sarli and others.

Singers Armando Laborde, Jorge Valdez, Mario Bustos, Osvaldo Lemos, Horacio Palma and a couple of others take us through to the end of the 1950s decade and beyond – all super powerful voices, but with mixed results from the dancer's perspective, not due to the singing but because tango in this era was floating back up from the feet to the ears.

Musicians

Over the decades of D'Arienzo's recording history there were several significant changes of influential musicians. The main periods of these changes can be simplified as:

1935 to 1939
Alfredo Mazzeo, who joined in 1928, became the principle violinist responsible for the ever-present 'buzzing bee' 4th string.

Domingo Mancuso was one of the other violinists during this period, and is particularly noted for working with pianist Rodolfo Biagi in 1937 to transform Pintin Castellano's composition *La Puñalada* from a pedestrian tango to a hit milonga. Canaro's release of the original tango version two months later was much less successful.

In 1935 the pianist in the orchestra was Lidio Fasoli, but it seems that he was often absent or late, so D'Arienzo turned to Luis Visca (his previous co-leader in the D'Arienzo-Visca sextet) but Visca too, with a history of fragile behaviour, had a tendency of not showing up for performances.

Rodolfo Biagi, having recently completed a tour of Brazil with the orchestra of Juan Canaro, was available for work. He was a friend of D'Arienzo, and frequently in the audience of the Chantecler Club. The existence of rhythmical tango that we dance to today is due to Biagi being asked to stand in for an unreliable Visca who had failed to stand in for an unreliable Fasoli! Biagi soon became the orchestra's most influential pianist.

This rapid turnover of pianists raises the question of who was playing the piano in the 1935 recordings, particularly in the later months. All credits currently go to Fasoli for the first five studio sessions, from 2nd July 1935 to 12th December 1935, with Biagi first recording on 31st December 1935. If this is correct, then Fasoli was obviously more conscientious about turning up for his recording obligations than for his club performances.

There is a compelling line of thought that the creator of the D'Arienzo sound was not really D'Arienzo, but Biagi. It is probably more balanced to say that D'Arienzo was warming up to a style that Biagi set ablaze. There is more about Biagi under his own section later, but suffice to say that the short, sharp punctuated piano notes from late 1935 to mid 1938 are his. Listen to:

  * *La Puñalada* (1937)

By 1938 D'Arienzo had come to resent the increasing popularity of Biagi who had, unwittingly, become the star of the show. Just as the orchestra leader refused to allow his singers to be the centre of attention, he was not going to be outshone by his pianist. Biagi had to go. He was replaced briefly by Juan Polito who emulated Biagi's signature style. Biagi had gone, but his presence in the D'Arienzo sound had not. Listen to

  * *Mandria* (1939)

The bandoneón engine drivers during the 1935-39 period include Juan Visciglio, composer of the well known D'Arienzo recordings *Pensalo Bien* (1938) and *Que Dios Te Ayude* (1939) , and Domingo Moro composer of *Ansiedad* (1938). Both had been with D'Arienzo since the late 1920s.

The double bass player during those years was Rodolfo Duclós, who contributed his own composition to the list of D'Arienzo recording hits, the excellent vals *Recuerdos de la Pampa* (1938).

1940 to 1950

At the end of 1939 most of D'Arienzo's musicians left the orchestra. Despite commercial success and widespread popularity they could no longer tolerate the internal tensions, most likely aggravated by D'Arienzo's aloof management style. They collectively resigned giving the contractual notice of one month.

Such a comprehensive departure could have had a devastating effect on D'Arienzo's successful, high profile status in the tango world. However, he maintained a publicly positive profile and immediately set about building a new orchestra. He did this quickly by taking control of the existing orchestra of Héctor Varela – making Varela his musical arranger and lead bandoneonist. Varela was the co-composer with D'Arienzo of several tangos, for example *Lo Mismo Que Ayer* (1946).

Additionally D'Arienzo recruited the pianist Fulvio Salamanca who was a skilled and imaginative pianist playing from the soul. Whilst there are similarities to the Biagi staccato style he has a more commanding power that controls the whole track. Listen to:

* *La Cumparsita* (1943)

D'Arienzo recruited from the De Caro orchestra the virtuoso violinist Cayetano Puglisi who took responsibility for the 'buzzing bee' signature sound. You can watch him have his moment in the YouTube clip of *La Cumparsit*a on Uruguayan television (1961).

<u>1950s onwards</u>
Varela left in 1950 and was replaced by Carlos Lazzari (from a long pedigree of orchestras including Canaro and Caló). He become lead bandoneonist and musical arranger right through to the end in 1975. In 1957 pianist Salamanca left and was replaced by Juan Polito, in his third appearance as the D'Arienzo pianist. And due to deteriorating health in 1968 Puglisi's position as lead violinist was taken by Bernardo Weber, who diligently continued the 4th string buzzing bee signature sound.

D'Arienzo Summary

- King of the Beat
- Theatrical conductor
- Buzzing bee violin
- Choppy piano

Rodolfo Biagi

Personal Story

Rodolfo Biagi was born in 1906 in the neighbourhood of San Telmo in Buenos Aires. Unusually among the tango maestros, none of his family members was gifted musically nor linked to music, but early on in his music lessons at school he became hooked. He later recalled making such a fuss about getting a violin that, despite his parent's attempts to discourage him, they eventually gave in, buying him one and signing him up to a music school. His teacher soon noticed that he was not a natural violinist, but more suited to the piano, much to the continued concerns and doubts of his parents.

His talent was such that by the age of thirteen he had qualified as a piano teacher himself and was playing at local cinemas, providing music for silent films. Two years later he was recruited by the pioneer tango maestro and recording star Juan Maglio.

In 1930 he was invited to accompany the great Carlos Gardel, who until then had sung only accompanied by guitars. Biagi was to be his first pianist! The recordings reveal that he had not yet created, or was not permitted to play, his signature staccato style. The short, distinct pieces of Biagi keyboard at this time are quite sweet compared to the frenetic energy of his playing some five or six years later.

For the next few years Biagi continued building his style until 1935 when he took his chance one night to fill the empty seat of D'Arienzo's notoriously unreliable pianists (see the section on D'Arienzo's musicians). From that night, the path of both D'Arienzo and Biagi was set. Their explosively successful relationship took tango backwards in terms of aesthetic sophistication, but irrepressibly forwards in terms of the popular dance culture.

The winning formula ended abruptly with Biagi's dismissal in 1938 (for being far too popular), but Biagi wasted no time in forming his own orchestra in the same year.

Biagi is often associated with the nickname Manos Brujas (Bewitched Hands), and one could be forgiven for thinking that he was so called because of his wizardry with D'Arienzo. However, he actually picked up that label later once he had formed his own orchestra in 1938. He began every performance, particularly on Radio Belgrano, with the 1929 foxtrot '*Manos Brujas*'.

Rodolfo Biagi was a successful composer as well as pianist and orchestra leader, and his work included the much loved *Gólgota* (also recorded by Lomuto); *Humillació*n and *Indiferencia* (also recorded by D'Arienzo); and *Campo Afuera* (also recorded by Donato).

Signature Sounds

Biagi's overall sound is characterised by Biagi himself, dominant on the piano. He said that he had never been able to accept the role of the piano in tango orchestras as one of accompaniment, and that it was not until he played for D'Arienzo that he could really let himself fly.

His style of playing can be described by consulting all of the synonyms in a thesaurus for hammering. The piano punctuates the phrases in impatient staccato bursts, and with unexpected off-beat timings, in a style that no regular tango composer nor arranger would or even could design. This came from deep within him. Commentators often refer to his playing as mad, possessed or (in the case of tango historian José Gobello) 'almost epileptic'.

D'Arienzo had attracted the name of King of the Beat, and Biagi deserves his title - King of the Off-Beat. His crazy, unpredictable off-beats were his classic signature sound from 1938 to the early 1940s. Every dancer expects an emphasis on the first and third beat, even if there are some syncopated beats or double time in between. To omit them and to emphasise the second and fourth instead seems like madness. The effect is not just that the first and third are omitted, but that he uses the silences like strong beats. If you examine a waveform analysis of a Biagi tango between 1938 and 1940, you will notice how prominent the silences are.

He catches out even the most experienced dancers, regardless of how many times they have listened to his music, because his beats are so counter-intuitive. Listen to:

* *Bélgica* (1942)

Like most orchestras, Biagi changed his style in the mid 1940s, reducing his reliance on emphasised off-beats, slowing down, and allowing the singers more time and prominence. Listen to:

* *Lucienne* (1946)

In this you can appreciate the deep, rich tones of the violin and the melody of Alberto Amor's voice.

Singers

Biagi's first singer was a safe pair of hands, or vocal chords, in the form of Teófilo Ibáñez. This singer had been around for a long time and was an established voice and personality in the Old Guard tango world, and as such, was Biagi's surest early route to the buying public. Ibáñez had made about one hundred and forty recordings with Firpo in 1928 alone, then more with Carabelli, with the Orquestas Típicas Victor, Porteña, and Brunswick, and with De Caro, Donato, and Fresedo. Listen to:

    * *Gólgota* (1938)

Andrés Falgás came next and recorded some of the most popular Biagi valses that we hear today. Listen to:

    * *Dichas Que Vivi* (1939)

Falgás composed *Tu Voz,* later recorded in 1944 by Biagi with singer Carlos Acuña.

Jorge Ortiz had previously been singing and recording tangos for Donato and others. He joined Biagi in 1939 and recorded a relatively modest thirty-nine tracks, yet created in the minds of the listening public an inseparable single entity - Biagi/Ortiz. Ortiz had a big stage personality and brought not just rhythm but emotion to Biagi's music. Listen to:

    * *Humillación* (1941)

Ortiz broke from Biagi and tried his luck with Miguel Caló. When that did not work out, he went on tour in South America and, although he limped back to Biagi years later, it was too late to replicate the previous success.

With the change in style in the 1940s, as the melodies slowed down and the singers became more dominant, Biagi's singers from 1943 included Carlos Acuña, Alberto Amor, Carlos Saavedra, Hugo Duval, and Carlos Almagro. Listen to:
   * *Adiós Te Vas* (1943) with Acuña;
   * *Paloma* (1945) with Amor;
   * *Alguien* (1956) with Duval.
Duval's voice has an oscillation that is augmented by the vibrating violins and bandoneóns, creating a new signature sound for the 1950s.

In 1970, Duval sang with the Trio Yumba that sounds like, and is often mistaken for, Biagi but Biagi had died the year before.

Musicians

Biagi the pianist is the star, ever present with decorative flourishes, a steady thumping beat and unexpected emphases.

Throughout the two decades of his recordings there are some lovely pieces on violin and bandoneón, but it is unclear who is producing those sounds. During the period 1938 to 1956, some of the main musicians who spent time in the orchestra included: bandoneonists Alfredo Attadía, Miguel Bonano (formerly with Donato) and Ricardo Pedevilla; and violinists Marcos Larrosa, Claudio Gonzalez and Oscar de la Fuente.

Without knowing specifically who played on particular recordings we can still appreciate the violinist in *Dichas Que Vivi* (1939) and *Pájaro Herido* (1941) and the bandoneonist in *Flor de Montserrat* (1945).

Biagi Summary

• Energetic pianist
• King of the Off-Beat
• Unexpected silences cause happy faux pas on the dance floor!

Ricardo Tanturi

Personal Story

Ricardo Tanturi was born in Buenos Aires in 1905. Music was part of his family life. When Ricardo was studying violin as a child, his elder brother Antonio was already co-leader of the tango Orquesta Típica Tanturi/Petrone. It was Antonio who convinced young Ricardo to change from violin, and who taught him to play the piano.

By the time Ricardo was nineteen the two brothers were playing on Radio Nacional, but despite Antonio's influence Ricardo was more interested in jazz and his studies at the Faculty of Medicine. However he must have been persuaded, because by 1933, at the age of twenty-six, he formed his first sextet, Los Indios – not a reference to the native Indian or creole history of Argentina, as is often assumed, but a homage to his favourite polo team. He performed successfully at high profile venues and, in 1937, he secured his first recording contract with Odeon. Unfortunately Odeon appears to have had a strategy of signing up promising new orchestras in order to prevent them going to their competitors, namely Victor Records. And then restricting their output so as not to compete with

Odeon's own star performers. In this way they restricted Tanturi's output to one disc per year: *Tierrita* (1937) and *Gallo Ciego* (1938). Troilo later suffered a similar 'one disc per year' fate with Odeon.

In 1940, as soon as he could, Tanturi signed with the Victor label and remained with them throughout the main tango dance period to the 1950s. It was from 1941 to 1943 that his popularity really took off, in large part due to the recruitment of the singer Alberto Castillo. When Castillo left to pursue a solo career, Tanturi, fearing the collapse of his own orchestra, acted quickly. He augmented his line-up, adding two bandoneóns, two violins, and brought in a replacement singer, thereby creating his most enduring and popular sound that lasted until at least 1945.

His reliance on his singers is reflected by the low number of instrumentals recorded. From 1937 to 1950 he made one hundred and forty-five recordings, only sixteen of which were instrumental, the majority of those being recorded in his early years to 1941.

As well as the being orchestra leader, Ricardo Tanturi was a composer of tango, vals, and milonga, including his dance classic *Pocas Palabras* and the milonga *Mozo Guapo*. He did not record his composition *Que Importa,* but there is popular version by D'Arienzo/Echagüe (1939).

Signature Sounds

The centre of the sound is the piano, Tanturi's instrument. But it is not Tanturi playing – it is Armando Posada who joined in 1936 when Tanturi grew his sextet and took up the orchestra leader's baton.

The tango author Michael Lavocah describes Tanturi's music as 'muscular'. Tanturi certainly knew how to thump out a good dance tune and get people up dancing. However, the piano is more than the thumping beat, and often decorates. Listen to:

  * *Comparsa Criollo* (1941) between 10 and 30 seconds;
  * *El Buey Solo* (1941) and its gentle introduction.

Turning to the overall sound of the orchestra, there are similarities in feel with D'Arienzo's music. There is a pronounced rhythmic beat, short sharp piano punctuating the phrases, and low violin over the choppy rhythm. Listen to:

  * *Comparsa Criolla* (1941);
  * *Pocas Palabras.* (1941)

These are both by the orchestra of Tanturi but you would be forgiven if you mistook them for D'Arienzo.

One main point of difference between them is that the violins are more prominent in Tanturi than in D'Arienzo, for example in *Comparsa Criolla*.

Rhythmic: Tanturi

Although there are often lovely individual violin and bandoneon pieces (by players covered in the Musicians section) they are neither distinct enough, nor consistent enough, to be called signature sounds.

Sometimes when trying to identify an orchestra we have to wait for the signature sound... and in Tanturi's case we have to wait until the very end. As the tango is finishing, you can expect the traditional "chan chan" ending but Tanturi makes us wait for the final note of resolution: Chan... (wait for it)... chan. Listen to the end of:

* *Pocas Palabras* (1941)

Singers

Although Tanturi's musicians were very good at what they did, he did not have any virtuoso stars, and so what he needed, and found, was an outstanding singer.

This person arrived in April 1939 in the shape of Alberto Salvador De Lucca, already on the tango scene with orchestras such as Julio De Caro, but performing under the names of Carlos Duval and Alberto Dual. Renamed again as Alberto Castillo, he first recorded with Tanturi in January 1941. He was an unusual tango singer, putting emphasis in different parts of his phrasing as if personally addressing the audience and the dancers. He was primarily a showman, as theatrical in his gestures as in his singing, and he quickly attracted a large and enthusiastic fan base. Listen to:

* *Asi Se Baila El Tango* (1942)

When performing this tango live, he infamously sang with dismissive gestures to the dancers around him when singing the lyrics 'What do the snobs, the emaciated and the fops know? What do they know what tango is? What do they know about rhythm?' On at least one occasion his audience interaction resulted in a near riot!

In the early days with the Tanturi orchestra Castillo tried to maintain his daytime profession as a gynaecologist, but the time pressures were such, together with a waiting room becoming fuller and fuller with healthy young women eager to see their idol, that he gave up his medical career to focus on singing.

The charismatic Castillo soon had his eyes on a solo career, and in mid-1943 he told Tanturi that he was leaving. Tanturi, fearing the end of his own career, did not handle the situation well and furiously predicted, wrongly, that Castillo would be a hopeless failure without him.

Fortunately they both continued to be separately successful. Tanturi was rescued by a cliché, 'as one door closes another opens', when he found the established and popular Uruguayan Enrique Inocencia Troncone, performing under the stage name of Ruiz. To avoid any confusion with Fresedo's Ricardo Ruiz, Tanturi turned to a random page in the telephone directory and renamed him Enrique Campos!

Campos did not have the individualistic stage presence of Castillo but in many ways he blended better, both vocally and personally, with the orchestra. Listen to:
   * *La Abandoné y No Sabía* (1944)

After Campos came Osvaldo Ribó, whose style was to hold notes for a long, long time – probably just too long for most dancers to feel comfortable. Listen to:
   * *Remembranza* (1947) particularly at 2 minutes 6 seconds.

Musicians

There were neither star performers nor any particular individuals responsible for the signature sounds, other than the pianist, Armando Posada. However, worthy of note is Vicente Salerno, Tanturi's first violinist, who was with him from the first recordings in 1937 through to the late 1950s. We can hear Salerno on one of his own numerous compositions: *La Serenata* (1941).

Another long serving musician was José Raúl Iglesias, bandoneonist. He was a composer too, and provided Tanturi with many hugely popular recordings such as the valses *Mi Romance* (1941) and *Al Pasar* (1943), and the tango *Igual Que Un Bandoneón* (1944). However, it was Héctor Gondre who became Tanturi's main bandoneonist who can be heard making short bursts of decorations, for example in *Con Los Amigos* (1943).

The long-service award must go to bandoneonist Francisco Ferraro. He started with Ricardo's brother Antonio in the 1920s, shortly after he joined Ricardo and stayed until 1950.

Tanturi Summary

- Dominant thumping piano
- Wait for the ending: Chan... (delay)... chan

Enrique Rodríguez

Personal Story

Aquilino Enrique Rodríguez Ruiz was born near Buenos Aires in 1901. His music studies led him to the bandoneón, and like many young musicians he played at local cinemas, accompanying the piano player during silent films.

In the 1920s he supported a number of orchestras, on the way to forming his own, but it was not until comparatively late in life, in his late twenties, that he played in the famous tango orchestra of Edgardo Donato. It was this experience that was to influence his sharp, rhythmic dance style, to which he added a healthy mix of musical fun.

In 1936 he assembled the 'Orquesta de Todos Los Ritmos' (Orchestra of all Rhythms). He had cannily decided not to form yet another tango orquesta típica, but to become the chosen outfit for organisers who could not afford several specialist orchestras for one event. He would play tango, foxtrot, polka, jazz, anything and everything. It was a shrewd and commercially successful move.

In 1937 he was contracted by the record company Odeon and stayed with them through to 1971, recording right up to two months before he died. It is a credit to Rodríguez's popularity and commercial success that he was part of the star line-up to celebrate the twenty-first anniversary of the Odeon record company at the famous Buenos Aires stadium of Luna Park, in October 1944. The artists playing were Canaro, Biagi, Caló, and Rodríguez.

Amongst some three hundred and fifty recordings with Odeon, only about half were tango, vals or milonga. It is because of this musical diversity that Rodríguez is often overlooked as a tango maestro but, by his own design, he was not a tango purist. It is interesting that there does not appear to be same dismissive feelings for Orquesta Típica Victor, who recorded over ninety non-tango rhythms, nor for the diverse portfolios of Canaro, Lomuto, Donato, D'Arienzo and others.

Rodríguez is not known as a tango composer, yet amongst many original compositions he created the very danceable *En La Buena Y En La Mala*; *Llorar Por Una Mujer*; *Como Has Cambiado Pebeta*; *Son Cosas del Bandoneón* (also recorded by Biagi and Lomuto); and the comic vals *Tengo Mil Novias.*

Signature Sounds

The overall feel of Rodríguez's music is one of simple rhythms - happy and upbeat. The positive feel is an influence from his time with Donato, and the choppy bandoneón rhythms have similarities to both D'Arienzo and Biagi. Listen in particular to the start and end of:

 * *Danza Maligna* (1940)

Danza Maligna starts with off-beats and unexpected missed beats, and is punctuated with sharp, staccato piano – who does this remind you of? Biagi, of course! Now listen to the end part of D'Arienzo's *Pensalo Bien* (1938) and Rodríguez's *Danza Maligna* (1940). They seem almost identical in the bandoneón flourish.

The most effective signature sound, however, is what is *not* there - the final note of resolution. Listen again to the end of *Danza Maligna,* and then check many of the other tracks in your Rodríguez collection. He often leaves us hanging, waiting for the final resting note, and, more often than not, it does not come. In other words, instead of the traditional ending of 'Chan chan' we hear 'Chan...' (that is it!). It is at that point that many dancers look at each other and say "Rodríguez!"

If we listen closely to other Rodríguez tangos there is sometimes a final note of resolution, but it is extremely weak, so the effect is much the same: 'Chan...'.

There is a line of thought that Rodríguez may have always played the final note but delayed it, like Tanturi, and then for some unknown reason the recording, or the transfers of the recordings, have been cut short. However, the missing or weak final note is entirely consistent with the fun style of Rodríguez, and we can be fairly sure that he would smile to hear the surprised laughter of dancers missing the ending.

In 1944 Rodríguez started to tinker with his successful formula, replacing his main musicians. He brought in Roberto Garza as lead bandoneonist and musical director. The orchestra moved to a softer, less rhythmic sound that was still able to produce some great dance tunes, such as the 1945 *Luna Llena* and *Tu Intimo Secreto*.

We sometimes hear Rodríguez foxtrots played today, replacing the milonga tanda. Many dancers love them as a happy release from the restraints of tango technique, but, of course, many do not! In his non-tango tracks Rodríguez used instruments not generally heard in his tangos – instruments most often associated with the signature sounds of other tango orchestras. Listen to three of his most commonly played foxtrots, for example *La Colegiala*, *Para Mi Eres Divina* and *Noches de Hungria,* and you will hear woodwind, cymbals, drums, and all manner of exciting sounds.

Singers

On Rodríguez's first record in November 1937 Roberto 'El Chato' Flores featured as the singer. The nickname 'El Chato' means a large, squashed nose. Flores featured on all but one of the thirty-four recordings made until December 1939, and became a significant part of the Rodríguez sound and character. In keeping with the Orquesta de Todos Los Ritmos, his first recording with Rodríguez was a foxtrot and his last was a pasodoble. There were twelve 'other rhythms' recorded, including foxtrot, pasodoble, marcha and ranchera. Flores was immediately popular and successful with his enjoyable tangos and valses too. Listen to:

* *Tengo Mil Novias* (1939);
* *Son Cosas del Bandoneón* (1939).

At the end of 1939 Rodríguez's own record label, Odeon, effectively poached Flores to promote him as a solo singing star. Armando Moreno, aged only eighteen, replaced Flores, making his first recordings in March 1940. Rodríguez reiterated his orchestra's point of difference by again making the first recording an 'other rhythm' – a pasodoble – with a tango on the B-side.

Due to his young age Moreno was known as El Niño, 'The Boy', and the nickname stayed with him throughout his twenties. El Niño remained with Rodríguez until January 1946, featuring on all but nine of the one hundred and forty tracks that Rodriguez recorded. The balance of instrumentals to those with a singer is a clear indication of the reliance of Rodríguez on the voice in the absence of any particularly talented musicians to make outstanding instrumentals. Listen to:

* *En La Buena Y En La Mala* (1940);
* *Yo No Se Porque Razon* (1942).

Although Moreno left in 1946 he returned to record with Rodríguez over a decade later.

There were several other singers after 1946, such as Ricardo Herrera, Fernando Reyes and Omar Quiros, but they do not hit the spot like Flores and Moreno, and so are rarely heard at today's milongas.

Musicians

Rodríguez's main dance music years lasted from the formation of the orchestra in 1936 to the mid 1940s, during which time the core line-up remained stable.

Eusebio Giorno was the pianist, the musical arranger of the orchestra and an occasional composer. Many years earlier he had composed the beautiful vals *Con Tu Mirar,* recorded by Rodríguez with Moreno in 1941. We can hear clearly that it is Giorno's piano carrying the tune along. His important contribution to the orchestra is tinged with sadness, and probably bitterness. Giorno's son, Jorge, claimed years later that the musical brain in the orchestra was his father, and that when Rodríguez changed his orchestra in 1944 his father was unceremoniously dismissed – and, as result, he chose never to play the piano again.

The lead violinist Carlos Pampillón was also a composer, responsible for the popular *Yo No Se Por Que Razón* (recorded by Rodríguez in 1942). On this, and other tracks, the lead bandoneonist, José Pane, plays the closing flourishes.

Rodríguez Summary

- Happy, upbeat feel
- Ending is withheld: Chan...

Ricardo Malerba

Personal Story

Ricardo Malerba was born in the Buenos Aires barrio of Parque Patricios in 1905. He came from a musical family. His two brothers, Alfredo and Carlos, both became tango musicians, and the three of them worked and toured together as young men. This included a trip to Europe as part of the orchestra of Cátulo Castillo, alongside Miguel Caló and the singer Roberto Maida. The brothers stayed on in Europe as a trio, with Alfredo on piano, Carlos on violin and Ricardo on bandoneón. Sadly, in 1931 Carlos died suddenly. At his funeral in Spain, Roberto Maida sang one of Carlos' favourite tangos. As an indication of tango's enduring friendships and loyalties, some thirteen years later Maida's younger brother, Antonio, would be singing and recording with Ricardo Malerba's orchestra.

Once the two remaining brothers returned to Buenos Aires, Alfredo had an overt live-in love affair with the already married tango and film star Libertad Lamarque. They went on to marry in 1945.

The relationship proved to be a happy event for Ricardo too. In 1938 his influential sister-in-law-to-be arranged a regular slot for him on the prestigious Radio Belgrano. Libertad was a fan of the music of D'Arienzo, so it should be no surprise that Ricardo's orchestra reflected D'Arienzo, whose rhythmic sound was in vogue at the time. Given the new family connection to Libertad Lamarque, it may not have been entirely on his own merit that Ricardo found himself in the film business, appearing in 'La Vida de Carlos Gardel' (released in 1939). His brother Alfredo, lover of the famous film star, composed the music score for the film. Malerba performed 'Noches de Montmartre' in the film, a tango that he later made as his first recording in September 1941. He can also be seen in the film 'Cita En La Frontera' (1940) starring, of course, Libertad Lamarque.

A year passed before Ricardo's second time in the studio. He recorded just two discs in 1942, then a further twenty-two over the next two years, and – as far as his dance music period is concerned – a final two tracks in 1945.

Ricardo Malerba also composed several of his most popular dance recordings, such as La Piba de los Jasmines (tango), Mariana (milonga) and Cuando Floreczan Las Rosas (vals). His co-composer on many, and co-arranger of all, was his pianist and friend Dante Smurra.

Signature Sounds

When Ricardo was contracted to play on Radio Belgrano in 1938 he was encouraged to emulate the popular style of Juan D'Arienzo. During his earlier recordings, with singer Orlando Medina, we can hear the similarities. But Malerba is not a cover band copying the hits of others. Both he and his pianist Dante Smurra developed their own style, recording many of their own compositions.

However, there is no denying the influence of D'Arienzo. Listen to Malerba's first recording, from the film '*La Vida de Carlos Gardel*':
* *Noches de Montmartre* (1941)
The staccato rhythm and the signature slow, low violin could easily be mistaken for D'Arienzo.

In 1943 we can recognise the style similarities between D'Arienzo/Mauré in *Enamorado* and Malerba/Medina in E*mbrujamiento*. The latter, composed by Malerba and Smurra, was recorded by D'Arienzo first in 1942. It feels as though it was composed and arranged especially for D'Arienzo, since it had the D'Arienzo feel and signature sounds. The Malerba and Medina version five months later had the same features but is stronger both musically and vocally. On the other side of the recording of this disc was the beautiful *Remembranza*. Here it is evident that Malerba had found his own sound. Track for track, during 1942 I would say that he outshone D'Arienzo.

The attraction of the Malerba sound is that he builds on the D'Arienzo rhythm but then, unlike D'Arienzo, puts more emphasis on the melody line and on the singer's delivery, while his violins often soar above the low drone. Listen to:

* *Oiga, Mozo* (1942) at one minute seventeen seconds.

Singers

Malerba recorded with four singers, but the main focus is on his first, Orlando Medina, who sang on the first recording in September 1941 and continued through to September 1944 – those being Malerba's main dance years.

His voice is strong and clear, and ideally suited to rhythmic dance music. In an interview he reveals a regret that he was not chosen by Juan D'Arienzo – particularly as, prior to 1941, he was playing with, and was a close friend of, Héctor Varela, who in the 1940s was D'Arienzo's lead bandoneonist and musical arranger. D'Arienzo/Medina could have been a spectacular match, and Medina believed it would have been. Notwithstanding, he left several very fine recordings with Malerba that still get the dance floors busy. Listen to:

   * *Gitana Rusa* (1942)

There was a seamless transition in September 1944 from Medina to Antonio Maida (the younger brother of the better known Roberto), when Maida recorded the A Side and Medina the B Side. Maida left for a solo career in 1946. Listen to:

   * *Encuentro* (1944)

Musicians

Despite the relatively short recording period, the partnership of Ricardo Malerba and his pianist Dante Smurra continued for several decades.

During the years that interest us most, between 1941 and 1945, Dante was co-arranger and co-composer with Malerba, and together they conceived, arranged, and recorded some of their greatest dance tracks. We can hear Dante's piano, often Biagi-like, with staccato bridging between phrases, in *La Piba de los Jasmines*; *Cuando Floreczan Las Rosas*; *Embrujamiento and others*.

Malerba's lead violinist Alfredo Lattero was probably responsible for the low, slow violin that emulates D'Arienzo's Cayetano Puglisi. Lattero had earlier co-composed *No Mientas*, which was made famous by D'Arienzo in 1938.

Malerba Summary

• Helped by his brother Alfredo and famous filmstar sister-in-law Libertad Lamarque
• Limited recordings
• D'Arienzo-esque, with respect for the singer

PART THREE:
THE LYRICAL

Osvaldo Fresedo

Personal Story

Osvaldo Nicolas Fresedo was born in Buenos Aires in 1897 to an Italian father (a successful businessman) and Spanish mother (a music teacher). He grew up in a comfortable middle-class home learning the piano and listening to his parents' gramophone recordings of the tango pioneers.

In 1912 he saw Augusto Berto playing the bandoneón in a trio with violinist Francisco Canaro in a local café. He was so affected and inspired by this performance that he abandoned his business school studies to concentrate on his bandoneón lessons (much to the horror of his father, who expelled him from the family home). He then had to find work to support himself and, like Canaro, Firpo, and Berto he became a decorator.

His father soon made amends (unlike the terrible rift in the De Caro family), buying his son a bandoneón and welcoming him back to the Fresedo home. Osvaldo then teamed up with his brother Emilio on violin and a guitarist friend to perform as a tango trio around the bars and cafes of the neighbouring barrios. Earning himself a reputation as an accomplished bandoneonist, he gained the nickname El Pibe de la Paternal (the kid from the barrio Paternal).

By 1917 he was playing in the legendary carnival orchestra of Francisco Canaro and Roberto Firpo, and the following year was recording tangos, including his own compositions.

It is worth pausing to note that the huge popularity of tango in 1917 was built on the considerable success of talented, famous tango musicians over the previous couple of decades, before the recording era. And yet 1917 was still ten years before the earliest tangos that tend to be heard at today's milongas. One can only imagine the power and excitement created by the Firpo/Canaro carnival orchestra in this early era, with its numerous energetic young stars: two pianos (Firpo and Martinez), five bandoneóns (Fresedo, Arolas, Bachicha, Polito, and De Cicco), five violins (Canaro, Ferrazzano, Roccatagliata, Doutry, and Scotti), Bazan on clarinet, Michetti on flute, and Thompson on double bass. What a powerhouse of tango that must have been!

In 1920 the Victor record company sent Fresedo, Enrique Delfino, and Tito Roccatagliata to New York to record under the name Orquesta Típica Select. His time there was one of mixed fortunes. The good news was that he made some fifty recordings and had some success on the radio and in the New York cabarets. But tango, in the city obsessed by jazz, would only ever be a novelty attraction. This was epitomised by one cabaret owner who advertised them as Indians from the Pampas, and wanted Fresedo dressed as a gaucho. Enrique Delfino (the cultured, classical music loving composer and lyricist) had to sit half naked and tied to the piano leg as an 'Indian savage'. The trio soon returned to their beloved Buenos Aires.

At one point during the late 1920s Fresedo was operating several orchestras at the same time, all under the name of Fresedo, all playing on the same night at cinemas and cabarets across Buenos Aires. Although Fresedo himself would try to put in an appearance at every venue, each orchestra had a nominated manager. One of these was Carlos Di Sarli who, for the rest of his life, acknowledged Osvaldo Fresedo to be his true master, his 'Milonguero Viejo'. Julio De Caro and Miguel Caló were two more great orchestra leaders of the future who played under Fresedo.

Fresedo composed many beautiful tangos (the lyrics of which were written by his brother Emilio) such as *Canto de Amor, El Once, Siempre Es Carnaval, Sollozos* and *Vida Mia.*

Fresedo continued recording professionally until 1968. There are later 'Fresedo' orchestra recordings but he was not always present. He died in 1984.

Signature Sounds

Fresedo's recordings span four decades and his musical style changed accordingly. Osvaldo Fresedo had been playing and recording tangos very many years before he developed his style that is most commonly recognised by the twenty-first century milonga-goer. Due to sound quality challenges we tend to hear only a tiny fraction of his four hundred and fifty recordings made between 1926 and 1932. The early sextet sound is much more aligned to the Old Guard style and features Fresedo on a growling bandoneón. Listen to:

   * *Fumando Espero* (1927)

There was a brief interim period in 1931 when Fresedo's music became softer, more languid but had not yet developed to the most familiar sound associated with him today.

By 1933 his music had become more sophisticated and elegant, influenced by the jazz scene in North America (the big band cabaret jazz rather than the jazz of smoky downtown joints) and the music of the Hollywood era. It was there that Fresedo became attracted to the harp and the vibraphone. In order to identify his music it is easiest to listen out for those two unusual instruments:

   * *Isla de Capri* (1935)
   * *Como Aquella Princesa* (1937)

Very occasionally we can hear a vibraphone in other orchestras, for example in Caló's *El Vals Sonador* and OTV's *Temo* but these are rare guest appearances. In the same way Fresedo featured cymbals in a guest role, (although they are closely associated with Lomuto) for example in the soft romantic *Buscándote*.

In the 1940s Fresedo added an additional distinct sound to his recordings, the drums. He had included a drummer in his orchestras from as early as the 1920s, and continued to use drums in performances through the 1930s, but they did not form a distinct part of his recording sound. He begins to use them stridently during the era of singer Oscar Serpa, and particularly in the 1950s when Héctor Pacheco was singing. Listen to:

* *Ronda de Ases* (1942) when the drums make an unexpected announcement within the first five seconds;

* *Nostalgias* (1952) when they appear at eight seconds.

Singers

During the period of 1925 to 1931 Fresedo, almost inevitably, used the Old Guard singers Ernesto Famá, Teófilo Ibáñez, Agustín Magaldi, and the lesser known Juan Carlos Thorry. A few others, such as Luis and Roberto Díaz, made brief singing appearances with him in this early recording era. They sounded the same as they did singing with the other orchestras at the time and give no particular characteristic to the Fresedo sound.

1933 to 1939 is the main period for the Fresedo dance music heard at modern milongas. During that time the singer was Roberto Ray. Ray had recorded with Fresedo in 1931, but the orchestra sound was not yet the 'typical' Fresedo/Ray sound we know from 1933. It is then that Ray becomes known as the voice of Fresedo – he suited the new style of elegance and finesse. He is said to have had clear diction without any hint of porteño accent (from the working class port area of Buenos Aires), which differentiated him from other tango singers at that time. Listen to:
  Como Aquella Princessa (1937);
  Niebla de la Riachuelo (1937).

Ricardo Ruiz, Ray's replacement, had the same delicate vocal qualities that appealed to Fresedo. Ruiz was a sturdy masculine looking man, with a dapper moustache. He must have surprised many a member of the audience when he stepped in front of the orchestra to sing - as he opened his mouth, an unexpectedly high pitched, quite feminine voice emerged. Listen to:

Más Allá (1939);

Alas (1940).

Ruiz stayed until 1941, having recorded some twenty-eight tracks (including, rather surprisingly, a conga), and was replaced by Oscar Serpa, who recorded from 1942 to 1946. (Serpa later re-emerges with Di Sarli in the early fifties). Listen to Serpa in:

* *Jamás Retornarás* (1943)

There were later singers such as Carlos Mayel, Héctor Pacheco into the late 1950s and 1960s but they, and the music, hold little interest for the dancer.

Musicians

The Old Guard double bass player Humberto Constanzo was a stalwart member of Fresedo's orchestra throughout the dance years, as was second violinist Adolfo Muzzi, and bandoneonist Pascual Storti (composer of *Cordobesita*). Another bandoneonist, Luis Petrucelli (who we met as one of the orchestra founders of the Orquesta Típica Victor) was with Fresedo from 1936 until his untimely death in 1941.

The long-standing pianist from the 1920s' recordings was José Rizzuti. After a short break he returned to Fresedo in 1933 and can be seen playing the piano with Fresedo's orchestra in the film *'Tango!'* (1933). In 1939 Fresedo ended his contract with Radio Belgrano and moved to radio El Mundo. Rizzuti left the orchestra at this point as Radio Belgrano offered him a contract to perform with Roberto Ray.

The replacement pianist, coinciding with the arrival of singer Ricardo Ruiz, was Lalo Scalise. The best way to appreciate Scalise is to listen to one of his own compositions together with his lyrics, opening with him on the piano:

    * *Buscándote* (1941)

Harpists and vibraphone players are not usual in a tango orchestra, but as we have seen, they provide part of

Fresedo's signature sound. In *'Tango!'* Fresedo is seen conducting his orchestra, and there at the front is his harp, played by a woman whose name is not included in the film credits, but in all likelihood was his permanent harpist Nélida Geanneo.

As for the vibraphone player, until 1939 this was the resident percussionist Salomón Nisguritz, known as 'Don Saly', who was composer of many (not so famous) tangos. His replacement was de Luca, who also played both the drums and the vibraphone.

Fresedo Summary

- Refined upbringing reflected in his music
- Prolific and enduring
- Harp, vibraphone, percussion

Carlos Di Sarli

Personal Story

Miguel Di Sarli, widowed with three children, left the economic depression of Italy behind him for a new life in Uruguay. There he met Serafina Russomano. He married her and they had four more children – all boys. Due to conflict in Uruguay he feared for their safety, and so he moved with his wife and seven children to Argentina, setting up a gun shop in Bahía Blanca.

Miguel and Serafina had another two sons – first in 1903 came Cayetano and then Roque. Cayetano did not care for the old fashioned name his parents had given him, and so, from adolescence, he transformed himself in to a 'Carlos'.

Having learnt to play the piano he soon became attracted to the world of performing. At thirteen he ran off to be the pianist with a travelling group, without the knowledge of his distraught parents. Once back home, admonished, he was sent to La Pampa to play at a family friend's *confiteria* (tearoom/bar) and cinema, where he stayed for almost three years. This time away was the making of Carlos - the pianist, the tanguero, and the entertainer. He broke free from his classical repertoire and played all of his favourite tangos to enthusiastic, provincial audiences.

On his return to Bahía Blanca, aged sixteen, his musical plans were interrupted when he was shot in the eye. There are three versions of the story from the Di Sarli family. The first is that whilst the family was celebrating the imminent marriage of one of the brothers, Carlos entered his parents' shop where an employee accidentally fired a weapon. In the second version, the employee believed Carlos was a thief and deliberately fired. The third version is it that the young Carlos was hopelessly forlorn due to the unrequited love of a local girl, and, provoked by the coming wedding celebrations of his brother, shot himself.

Whatever the cause, the result was the loss of his sight in one eye, and the introduction of the trademark dark glasses.

Aged twenty he ventured to the big city of Buenos Aires, but he was not alone. He had family support in the shape of his uncle, the professional singer Tito Russomano, as well as family friend Alberico Spatola. The latter was the composer of the tango *El Trece,* and the musical director of the Buenos Aires Police Band, which played and recorded tangos. These two close family connections helped Carlos to secure work, including a placement in the successful tango orchestra of Anselmo Aieta.

He was also introduced to, and taken on by, Osvaldo Fresedo, who became his mentor and tango inspiration. Di Sarli composed *Milonguero Viejo* as a dedication to Fresedo, and remained grateful to him for the rest of his life. It is interesting to compare Fresedo's recordings from the mid to late 1920s with Di Sarli's enduring style. Fresedo's growling bandoneon has a similar effect to Di Sarli's later growling bass runs on the piano.

Di Sarli's superstar status in the modern tango era stands in harsh contrast with his troubled integration in to the tango *milieu* of Buenos Aires. His personal story is one of artistic brilliance and many personal kindnesses, but he frequently clashed with organisers and dominant figures in the tango scene. Juan D'Arienzo, for example, was openly hostile to him (although they warmed to each other much later in life). These episodes of conflict often led to his physical withdrawal, not just from his orchestra, but also from tango, and from the entire city of Buenos Aires. At those times the orchestra continued performing under his name, but would not make any recording. Di Sarli meanwhile sometimes travelled within Argentina, playing as the pianist for now lesser known orchestras. Other Di Sarli withdrawals were purely introverted – his musicians recall that he often seemed lost in a different place, remaining silent for long periods of time.

Some of the personality clashes Di Sarli experienced were due to his social awkwardness, and an inability to moderate his responses in challenging situations. A damaging example is revealed when he refused to perform for free at a charity event. This was not through any lack of generosity (his life story is full of acts of kindness) but, for whatever reason, he did not feel it was an appropriate proposition. The problem arose from the blunt manner of his refusal, and from his overall tendency to alienate himself from others, and it resulted in sustained nastiness by agitators in the tango business. It was not just disparaging comments, but also the sabotage of his live performances (with stage lights going out or sudden cancellation of venues, for example). It is clear that Carlos Di Sarli was an enigma, loved by many, misunderstood by many, and mistreated by some.

His recording history runs from 1928 to 1958, and amongst his own compositions were *Milonguero Viejo, Corazón, En Un Beso La Vida, La Capilla Blanca* and *Nido Gaucho*. He died aged fifty-seven in January 1960. Fittingly, his last performance in the previous March was his own composition *Bahía Blanca*, dedicated to his beloved hometown and frequent refuge.

Signature Sounds

The orchestra's most distinctive signature sound was Di Sarli's growling piano. It came from both hands, but it was his left hand, and his use of the pedals, which was a musical mystery at the time, and which remains so today. His piano music, if written down, was never shared nor did he allow others to see either what he was doing or how he did it. He positioned his piano so that his hands could not be seen. After his death, his friend Aníbal Troilo lamented that he had taken the secret to the grave. Troilo had also complimented Di Sarli's music in the 1950s, saying that it was truly of the old days, meaning it was pure and simple in the style of the 1920s and earlier.

Di Sarli often provides the rhythm to the violins' melody, and always links the phrases. Other orchestra leaders also do this but not so constantly. With Di Sarli, the piano is omnipresent, and, even though his arrangements and orchestration changed over the decades, the essence of his playing did not. The same characteristics can be heard in his recordings across four decades. Listen to:

* *El Paladin* (1929);
* *Corazón* (1939);
* *Ensueños* (1943);
* *Champagne Tango* (1952).

His piano keys often provide the first note in a track, although during a milonga (social dance) it may be hard to hear due to the buzz of conversation. Listen to:

    * *Bahía Blanca* (1957).

Likewise, he frequently closes a tango with piano notes, so it can often be worth waiting for the end of a track before coming to a conclusion about the orchestra. Listen to the piano closing note right at the end of:

    Don José Maria (1943 and 1954)

In his later era of the 1950s, he frequently adds a bell-like piano note, almost as a comma within the phrases. Listen to one minute and eleven seconds in:

    *Indio Manso (*1958)

The next instrument of major importance to Di Sarli's signature sound was the violin. He gave a full range to his violins, from staccato rhythm to legato melodies, but rarely as showcased pieces. The sound was full without exuberant virtuoso playing.

Di Sarli had an unusual attitude to the bandoneón, which is generally seen as the emblematic instrument of the tango sound. He said it was essentially an organ and so unsuitable for *firulete* (flowery adornments). Others thought differently (for example Pedro Laurenz). However, Di Sarli did not undervalue the bandoneón, he just used it in a different way, as explored in the *Musicians* section.

Singers

Of the twenty singers associated with Di Sarli we will focus on those that are most often heard at twenty-first century milongas. The main two singers with his sextet (1929 to 1931) were Santiago Devincenzi (sometimes known as Devin) and Ernesto Famá (see the chapter on Canaro for more on the latter). Although both perfectly good singers for the era, they were most renowned for their appearance - Devin for his heart-stopping good looks, and Famá for his tailored attire. Listen to:

    * *Cicatrices* (1930) with Devin
    * *Chau Pinela* (1930) with Famá.

There then followed a break of eight years before Di Sarli recorded again. In 1939 he recruited a very young Roberto Rufino, whose first performances with him at nightclubs were unlawful because he was under-age. Di Sarli resorted to covering the short-trousered youth in a long overcoat and standing him behind the piano. Following one of many disputes about this with a club owner Di Sarli secured a special dispensation from a judge that allowed Rufino to work in clubs at night.

The Di Sarli/Rufino partnership soon drew huge crowds, with fans, radio listeners and record buyers launching them both to tango stardom. Rufino stayed with Di Sarli for five years, singing on some forty-three recordings and describing that period as the most important in his life, crediting Di Sarli as his master, his second father, his adviser, and the greatest of gentlemen. Listen to:

* *Corazón* (1939)

At the height of Di Sarli/Rufino mania in 1940 you will notice a few recordings with other singers – Rodríguez Lesende and Agustín Volpe. They were covering Rufino's unavoidable absence whilst he was conscripted in to military service.

Then there was another landmark singer, Alberto Podestá (whose real name was Alejandro Washington Alé). He too was only seventeen years old when taken on by Di Sarli. Like Rufino, Podestá credits Di Sarli with being his finest mentor, artistically and personally.

Under the stage name Carlos Morel, the young Alejandro had already been performing and recording professionally with Miguel Caló. It was Di Sarli who renamed him Alberto Podestá, a stage name that would stay with him until he died in 2015. Podestá first recorded with Di Sarli in 1942, whilst still recording with Caló in the same year. In 1943 he recorded with Pedro Laurenz, but then returned to Di Sarli in March 1944. His most popular recordings with Di Sarli are from the years 1942 and 1944. Listen to:

* *Junto a Tu Corazón* (1942);
* *Tu!...El Cielo Y Tu!* (1944).

Podestá went solo in 1945, had a brief spell with Edgardo Donato, and returned for a second time to Di Sarli in 1947. His singing journey continued for decades, performing and recording with Francini-Pontier, Laurenz, Donato, and Caló again, amongst many others, almost to his final days, aged ninety-one.

Following Podestá came Jorge Durán in 1945, who was usually referred to as 'The Coffin'! According to the tango researcher Néstor Pinsón, this macabre nickname came from his habit of wearing an extra wide shouldered grey suit. Durán's most popular recordings were made in 1945. Listen to:

    * *Porteño y Bailarín*

Of the later singers, Oscar Serpa recorded once in 1948, but mainly between 1951 and 1955. Mario Pomar recorded between 1951 and 1955. (In the 1940s Pomar had recorded under his real name of Mario Corrales, including on the popular OTV vals *Temo*). Listen to:

    * *Verdemar* (1953) with Serpa;

    * *Nido Gaucho* (1955) with Pomar.

The years from 1954 to 1959 are best known for outstanding instrumentals, but also included recordings with Jorge Durán, Argentino Ledesma, Rodolfo Galé, and Horacio Casares.

Musicians

Di Sarli is always present on piano, though rarely as a showcase instrument. It is he who creates the mood and the dance drive, without any exuberant solos. He had instructed all of his musicians to leave the style to him.

Despite his difficulty in maintaining good relations with those in the business, he did have a number of loyal (and often long-suffering) musicians. His lead violinist Roberto Guisado, nicknamed Tierrita, stayed with him (on and off) for some thirty years from the early sextet days in 1929 through to 1956. His bandoneonist Félix Verdi served with him almost as long, joining in 1932 and remaining (again on and off) until 1956. He loved Di Sarli's treatment of the bandoneón, saying that it differed from anyone else's – the building crescendo and pumping staccato with the right hand, which would suddenly stop mid-chord allowing the violins to take over. For Verdi there was no finer master.

Di Sarli Summary

- Enigmatic outsider behind dark glasses
- Father figure to singers Ruffino and Podestá
- Piano starts, bridges, and ends
- Violins provide everything else

Miguel Caló

Personal Story

Miguel Caló was born in Buenos Aires in 1907 to Italian immigrant parents, the first born of an incredibly large family of seventeen children. As the eldest in those circumstances, he became responsible for earning money at an early age and, like Canaro, was driven to work hard and to succeed.

Having abandoned school to help support his brothers and sisters, he allowed himself a pleasure and a challenge. Without the knowledge of his parents he bought an old violin and secretly practised tango – until it was discovered and confiscated by his father. It was not that his parents were not musically inclined, but times were hard and serious work had to be done.

It is easy to imagine the tense domestic scene at that moment, but it was a drama happily resolved by Miguel's uncle, who gave him enough money to buy a bandoneón. Like so many of the leaders of our twenty tango orchestras, Miguel played at a cinema showing silent films, accompanying a pianist. He was so successful that he secured an eighteen-month contract. He was now able to bring a steady income in to the Caló

135

home. This changed his parents' views somewhat. They began to recognise that music was in the blood of their children, and supported them in their studies. Tango became the livelihood for five of the Caló siblings: (1) Miguel, of course; (2) Juan, who formed a sextet with Miguel in 1929, and later worked with (3) Francisco, the singer known as Roberto who led his own tango orchestra in the 1950s; (4) Armando, a bass player who played with Miguel; and (5) Antonio, a bass player who joined Miguel's orchestra in 1938. Another brother, Salvador, became a musician but took another route – he went to Miami, changed his name to Freddy, and became a very successful jazz bandleader.

Meanwhile Miguel was conscientiously improving his bandoneón playing and by 1926, aged nineteen, he had earned himself a seat amongst the bandoneonists of the prestigious orchestra of Osvaldo Fresedo. Within a few years he was touring, going to Spain in 1929 to team up with the Malerba brothers (Alfredo and Ricardo) and singer Roberto Maida, and in 1931 to the United States of America with Osvaldo Fresedo.

Miguel Caló had several attempts at leading his own orchestras, and, although they were short-lived, he did recruit many names that went on to become major figures in the tango world. This shows that he had a good eye and ear for talent. Some of his recruits included the pianists Osvaldo Pugliese, Horacio Salgán, Orlando Goñi (see the section on Troilo). On bandoneón he had recruited Astor Piazzolla, Domingo Federico, Armando Pontier and Juan Cambareri.

His first recording contract produced just one release, in 1932. It was with his orchestra from 1934 to 1938 that he laid down the roots for his rich melodic sound, with influences from his earlier maestro Osvaldo Fresedo. He recorded twenty-four tracks (including non-tango rhythms) with the well known singer Carlos Dante, the lesser known Alberto Morel, and for one record the very well known (to him at least) Roberto Caló, his brother.

Caló's most successful orchestra, recorded from 1941 to 1945 and comprised of young, up-and-coming talent. It became known as Orquesta de las Estrellas (Orchestra of the Stars). Thereafter, he continued successfully performing and recording with different line-ups in each decade, until his death in 1972.

He is remembered not just for his recordings, but also for the joint compositions with his pianist Osmar Maderna: *Qué Te Importa Que Te Llore*; *Jamás Retornarás*; and *Qué Falta Que Me Hacés!*

Signature Sounds

The overall feel of Caló's sound is rich and full, but not mellow. His lyrical sound seems to bounce along, accented by staccato violins giving rapid bursts of beat, and any smoothness in the sound is achieved largely by his choice of singers, particularly the crooner, Raúl Berón.

At times Caló can sound like Di Sarli, and on many occasions they released the same tangos, often very close in time to each other, for example:

* *Tarareando (*1942 Caló & Di Sarli);

* *Al Compás del Corazón (*April 1942 Caló & Di Sarli*)*;

* *Verdemar* (September 1943 Caló, October 1943 Di Sarli);

Caló's pianist, Osmar Moderna, bridges the phrases (just like Di Sarli) but is given much more prominence throughout the track than Di Sarli allows himself. Another point of difference is that Caló often uses the bandoneóns to pump out the rhythm, while Di Sarli prefers the violins. Listen to:

* *Cosas de Tango* (1945 Caló & Di Sarli 1946);

* *Nada* (1944 Caló & Di Sarli).

The lyrical phrases in Caló are often alternated with a clear staccato rhythm. Many orchestras play both the melody and rhythm together, two lines of music one over the other, both equally strong. Caló isolates his rhythm, dropping the melodic violins, and whereas some orchestras may occasionally use this technique too, Caló makes it a structural characteristic of his tangos. Listen to:

    * *Tristezas de la Calle Corrientes* (1942)

Caló's clearest signature sound is at the very end, and is a variation of the resolution. Like Tanturi, he makes us wait for the final note, and when it comes it is a piano broken chord: Chan...tring. But then, listen carefully, because that is not the end. Caló treats us to a single high note on the piano...ting! This Chan...tring...ting is a nice touch for the dancer to acknowledge.

Singers

When Caló was recording in the 1930s his singers included the ubiquitous Carlos Dante, and his own brother Roberto. However, the main period of interest for us is from 1940 with the orchestra that became the Orquesta de Las Estrellas.

Their first recording in 1941 featured the sixteen-year old singer Alberto Podestá, although he was not known by that name at the time. His real name was Alejandro Washington Alé. Caló decided to name him Juan Carlos Morel (after Caló's former singer, Alberto Morel, who had died young and suddenly). In the following year, when 'Juan Carlos Morel' moved on to Di Sarli's orchestra, Di Sarli renamed him Alberto Podestá.

Morel/Podestá would enjoy a higher profile and a higher salary with Di Sarli. But his departure left Caló greatly annoyed, and considered his move to be an act of great disloyalty having given him his first break, singing in clubs aged just fifteen.

On 9 April 1942 Di Sarli recorded *Al Compás del Corazón* with Podestá. Just twenty days later, on 29 April 1942, Caló (with his replacement singer Raúl Berón) also recorded *Al Compás del Corazón.* As wonderful as both versions are, it is the Caló and Berón version that made its mark. But why was this tango, which had never been recorded before, suddenly released twice?

The previous year, when Caló's orchestra was playing in a tearoom, his newly joined bandoneonist Federico Domingo played his own composition *Al Compás del Corazón* to his colleagues. Although both singers Berón and Podestá were present, it was the orchestra's violinist Enrique Francini who sang the lyrics. The tearoom audience loved it. When Podestá defected to Di Sarli soon after, he went armed with a potential hit – but Caló was not going to let him have a clear run.

However, Berón's recording debut of *Al Compás del Corazón* was a gamble that very nearly did not pay off. Michael Lavocah describes how Caló was pushed by his recording company to drop the crooning Berón, whose singing style was considered to be insufficiently tango-esque. Fortunately the rapidly increasing record sales saved their careers and treated us to a further two dozen or more delicious Caló/ Berón tracks.

Caló seemed to have had quite a fluid relationship with his singers. In 1943 Berón nipped off to record with Lucio Demare (less than successfully – see the *Singers* section in the chapter on Demare*)*. This gave Caló the opportunity to experiment. For example, one Friday in January 1943 the singer Jorge Ortiz was, as usual, recording with Biagi, but by the following Tuesday he was in the recording studio with Caló, with whom he stayed for five months. Ortiz returned to record with Biagi in 1945.

Podestá must have been forgiven for his desertion to Di Sarli, because he made a couple of later recordings for Caló in 1943, before leaving again for the orchestra of Pedro Laurenz (then coming back yet again in 1954).

To add to Raúl Berón came Caló's second Raúl - Raúl Iriarte. He had to abandon his real name Rafael Fiorentino (a perfectly stylish name for any tango singer) to avoid confusion with the already established Francisco Fiorentino. Iriarte remained with Caló until 1947, sharing the stardom in 1944 with Raúl Berón. The two Raúls went on to deliver the lyrics of Caló's finest collection of dance tracks.

The difference in tone that they each bring is a subtle one. Berón is a smooth, croony tenor while Iriarte uses a lower, more powerful voice. As we listen to their tracks the difference between the two singers becomes clearer. Listen to:
    * *Corazón No Le Hagas Caso* (1942) with Berón;
    * *Nada* (1944) with Iriarte.

Musicians

Caló, a bandoneonist, abandoned his instrument in 1940 when he formed his orchestra (later billed as Orquesta de Las Estrellas) to concentrate on conducting and managing his orchestra. He was not the creator but the enabler. His skill was to bring the finest musicians together, and rather than dictate from the front, he allowed them to be creative.

The bandoneóns you can hear are those of Armando Pontier and Domingo Federico. Pontier composed Caló's hits *Trenzas, Corazón No Le Hagas Caso, Margo* and *Tabaco.* He went on to co-lead an orchestra with Caló's violinist Enrique Francini, from 1946 to the 1970s, using, amongst other singers, Podestá and Berón. As for Domingo Federico, he composed Caló's hits *Al Compás del Corazón, Tristezas de la Calle Corrientes* and *Saludos.*

Until 1938 the lead violinist was Raúl Kaplún, who later became an influencing force in the sound of the orchestra of Lucio Demare.

The lead violinist on the recordings in the early 1940s was Enrique Francini. Among his many compositions are the Caló hits *La Vi Llegar, Mañana Ire Temprano* and *Azabache.*

Caló's pianist was Osmar Maderna, described by biographer Julio Nudler as the Chopin of Tango. Listen again to *Al Compás del Corazón,* focusing only on the piano throughout. Maderna is ever-present and a significant part of the overall Caló sound. Perhaps his presence is not surprising given that Maderna was the musical arranger. It is he too who provides the Caló signature ending of a closing broken chord and a single note - Chan...tring...ting. And, as mentioned earlier, Maderna co-composed several of Caló's hits: *Que Te Importa Que Te Llore, Jamás Retornarás* and *Que Falta Que Me Hacés!*

All good things must come to an end. By 1945 Maderna had left (after a blistering row with Caló) and gone too were Francini, Pontier, and Iriarte. There was a new line up that recorded in 1946, but from a dancer's perspective Caló's best years were over.

Maderna lost no time in forming his own successful orchestra, and he began recording the following year in 1946. However, any lasting success was denied him by tragedy. He was a keen pilot with his own light aircraft, and in April he became involved in an air race and manoeuvres with another pilot, each trying to outdo the other. The two aircraft collided and plummeted to earth. Both pilots and four on-board friends lost their lives. Maderna, the tango star, was dead at thirty-three years old. That tragic night, his pregnant wife Olga lost her baby.

Miguel Caló never forgot Maderna, and continued to admire his talent and contribution. In 1963 he recorded a tribute, his own composition *Para Osmar Maderna* – a dedication as simple as it is personal.

Caló Summary

- Alternate choppy and smooth phrases
- Smooth singers
- Distinct ending: Chan....tring....ting!

Lucio Demare

Personal Story

Lucio Demare was born in Buenos Aires in 1906. At the tender age of nine he earned money by playing piano on the ferryboats that continuously crossed the Río de la Plata between Buenos Aires and Montevideo. It is tempting to say that even when playing piano at such an early age, at least he knew that he was going places!

From the age of sixteen he began to play piano in jazz bands – the new music craze from the USA – including one in which he played alongside Juan D'Arienzo. Soon afterwards he was contracted to work in cabarets by the acclaimed jazz orchestra leader, Adolfo Carabelli. At that time he was not old enough to enter the cabaret premises legally, and had to have special permission from his mother to wear long trousers in order not to look so obviously underage!

Demare was able to get close to the Canaro orchestra because of his cousin, Luis Riccardi, who was Canaro's long serving pianist. Canaro's lead bandoneonist, Minotto Di Cicci, took him under his wing, and tutored him in the nature of tango music. Demare boldly asked

Francisco Canaro if he could accompany him on his forthcoming tour to Paris. At first Canaro rejected this idea, saying that a jazz pianist knew nothing of tango. Eventually Canaro relented (probably persuaded by Riccardi and Di Cicco), and in 1926 Demare went to Paris. He was accompanied by his father (a tango violinist), his mother and his brother, Lucas. Soon afterwards Francisco Canaro became the Demare family benefactor.

Whilst in Paris Demare became part of another Canaro enterprise. In 1928 Canaro put him together with two of his singers, Agustín Irusta and Roberto Fugazot, to form a trio. They went to Spain and had great success recording, and appearing in films. Over the years it became more and more complicated to maintain the momentum of the trio, and so in 1936 Demare returned home. He briefly re-joined the Canaro tango machine, where he was responsible for the musical arrangements and conducting the Canaro orchestra in theatre productions. Additionally he played in a piano duo with his cousin Luis Riccardi – Canaro's loyal pianist.

It was in 1938 that Lucio Demare put his own orchestra together, secured a recording contract with Odeon, and for the first time felt that he had found what he wanted to do - produce his own music, whether commercially lucrative or not. That was a perfectly sound protective strategy, given that Demare never achieved any wealth from his art. But he was happy.

In mid 1945 Demare closed down his orchestra to go on tour, reforming his old trio with Irusta and Fugazot. He recorded again in the 1950s, but the tracks are of less interest to the dancer.

Demare was the composer of the now world-famous *Malena* that, he proudly said, took him only fifteen minutes to write whilst sitting in a café. *Malena* has been recorded by numerous artists including Demare himself (three times), Miguel Caló, Francisco Canaro (twice), Aníbal Troilo (three times), and Osvaldo Pugliese.

Some of his other famous tango compositions include: *Mañana Zarpa Un Barco* (also recorded by Carlos Di Sarli); *Alas Rotas* (made famous by Edgardo Donato); *Solamente Ella* (also recorded by Di Sarli and by Francisco Lomuto); and *Más Allá* (recorded by Osvaldo Fresedo).

Signature Sounds

Demare's music flows as a whole and there are no musical specialities, no specific signature instruments nor musical tricks, nor outstanding musicians. And yet, despite those omissions, the music is divine.

The overall feel of Demare's music is lyrical and romantic. The construction is similar to that of Miguel Caló - rapid bursts of staccato violins contrasting with, but somehow not spoiling, the overall romantic feel. Demare's bursts of violin are not only short and sharp, like Caló, but often there is a rasp, producing a sound that is less pure. Listen to:

  * *Un Tango Guapo* (1942);
  * *Al Compás de Un Tango* (1942).

Demare was not an innovator, and his style has a mixture of influences. He identified his main influence as Francisco De Caro, sharing his aim of wanting to create a mood of lyrical romance. However, if we listen closely to the construction we can also detect the influence of his tango mentor, Canaro. There is simple repeated phrasing as the instruments follow each other, with little or no counter melodies, and the pace is steady, without complex changes in tempo.

In order to recognise Demare better we can compare the different styles of three versions of *Torrente*. Two were recorded in October 1944, the first by Troilo with singer

Alberto Marino, the second, a week later, by Demare with singer Horacio Quintana. The third *Torrente* was recorded in December that year by Canaro, with singer Carlos Roldán. When we listen to them in reverse chronological order they seem to get progressively more elaborate. Canaro, by now fifty-six years old, is less playful than he used to be, and his construction remains simple. Demare, thirty-eight years old, varies the phrasing by ranging between staccato and legato, and by changing the lead instrument between the violin, bandoneón, and piano. There is variety, but it is not complex. Troilo, only recently turned thirty, varies not just the rhythm and instrumentation, but also plays with the ebb and flow of the tempo.

There are many tangos recorded by both Demare and Troilo and by Demare and Tanturi. These are useful for comparing their different styles. Usually, Troilo is more complex, Tanturi more rhythmic and Demare more lyrical. Listen to:

   * *Y Siempre Igual* (Demare 1943 and Tanturi 1944);

   * *No Te Apures, Cara Blanca* (Demare 1942 and Troilo 1942).

Singers

In June 1938 Demare wanted a singer for his new orchestra, but he lacked confidence in his ability to make the right choice. He asked his mentor Francisco Canaro and his previous trio member Roberto Fugazot to each, separately, audition newcomer Juan Carlos Miranda. As if that was not enough of a trial for Miranda, immediately after the audition he was ushered straight into the studio to record *Telón* and *Din Don* – which remain amongst tango dancers' favourite Demare recordings.

Despite that promising rush of activity, Demare did not make any further recordings for another four years. His singer Miranda had to wait until December 1942 to record a set of tangos that are considered today to be classics, such as *Malena, Mañana Zarpa Un Barco, Pa'Mi Es Iqual, Al Compás de Un Tango* and *No Te Apures, Cara Blanca*.

During 1942 Demare had recruited Roberto Arrieta, a singer with an excellent background who had sung (but not recorded) with Carlos Di Sarli, Pedro Laurenz and other notable names. He recorded three tracks with Demare, including *Un Tango Guapo,* but at the end of the year Miranda decided to move on, perhaps concerned that he would have to wait a further four years before Demare's next session in the recording studio!

Demare now needed a replacement singer, and he enticed Raúl Berón away from the success he was enjoying with Miguel Caló. His recorded tangos with Demare include *Oigo Tu Voz* and *Tal Vez Sera Su Voz,* but Berón did not really match his own quality with Caló or the quality of Miranda with Demare.

In 1944 Demare was once again without a singer and found Horacio Quintana. They recorded a dozen tangos plus a vals and a milonga. Although perfectly respectable tracks, the collection presents limited opportunities for a tango DJ to play Demare/Quintana tandas (a set of three or four tangos), and so Miranda and Berón remain the singers most often heard.

Musicians

Demare himself led the orchestra from his piano, and so all of the piano notes we hear are his.

The main contributor to Demare's sound was his friend and bandoneonist Máximo Mori, known as 'Bocha'. He arranged Demare's first two recordings, *La Racha* and *Telón,* and stayed with Demare throughout his main recording period to 1945. They remained close friends until Lucio Demare's death in 1974.

In 1942 Demare was able to attract the violinist Raúl Kaplún, who composed and played on Demare's well known tracks *Una Emoción* (1943) and *Que Solo Estoy* (1944). The latter was also recorded by Di Sarli and by Pugliese. Kaplún was previously with the orchestra of Miguel Caló, recording with him from 1936 to 1938. During this time we can hear the familiar sound of scraping violin strings in short, sharp bursts, and we can hear him producing the same for Demare from 1942 onwards.

Demare Summary

• A protégé of Canaro
• Lyrical and romantic with scraping violins
• Composer of the classic tango 'Malena'

Angel D'Agostino

Personal Story

Angel Domingo Emilio D'Agostino was born in Buenos Aires in 1900 into a family of music lovers. Their home was regularly visited by tango composers and musicians, who gathered around the piano playing their favourite pieces. The composer Alfredo Bevilacqua brought his work *Independencia* (yet to be released publicly) to the house and performed it for the family. The young Angel D'Agostino, aged only eight years old, was offered the sheet music and played to great applause. A few years later it was recorded by Juan Maglio, and decades later it would be recorded, with great success, by Juan D'Arienzo.

At the age of eleven Angel D'Agostino performed on piano alongside violinist Juan D'Arienzo, as part of a youth theatre season, and from then on his life was dedicated to music, which ranged from classical to popular. When he was twenty he formed his own band and played a mixture of tango and jazz at renowned venues in the centre of Buenos Aires. By 1925 he was part of the Orquesta Típica Paramount, which played in the Paramount cinema, once more accompanying his violinist friend Juan D'Arienzo, amongst others.

He did not meet Angel Vargas, until 1932, when they briefly worked together. They followed separate careers and did not get together again until 1940, by which time D'Agostino had secured his first recording contract with Victor. At last the delighted tango world was treated to the magic of the Two Angels.

D'Agostino composed (jointly with his lead bandoneonist and musical arranger Alfredo Attadía) a couple of his own greatest tangos - *Tres Esquinas* and *El Cocherito*. And, alone, he composed his instrumental *Café Dominguez.*

In his personal life D'Agostino was a regular (and successful) poker player who mixed with the upper echelons of Argentine society. He was known as a good tango dancer and a determined bachelor, and although he enjoyed the company of many beautiful society women, mainly he enjoyed his own company, feeling uncomfortable with the fame that tango had brought him. His long time close friend and professional partner was the dapper poet/lyricist Enrique Cadícamo, and the two had vowed to live the life of unattached men of the world.

At the age of fifty, Cadícamo had something of a mid-life crisis and married a woman thirty years his junior. For D'Agostino, this was an act of treachery, and he never spoke to his closest friend again.

Signature Sounds

D'Agostino's music is subtle, and seems almost wistful. Although difficult for non-Spanish speakers to appreciate, his choice of tango lyrics is a clear identifying signature characteristic, being nostalgic and often about Buenos Aires. He arranged the vocals to fit the mood of the words - the voice of Angel Vargas is equally wistful. It is easy to imagine Vargas gazing into the middle distance, recalling years gone by, as he sings.

So if you are not yet fluent in Spanish, what else is there to identify the sound of D'Agostino? The biggest help can be found in his use of the Call and Response technique. This is a musical device that other tango orchestras frequently deploy, but only as a variation, a bit of fun, before moving on. D'Agostino uses it as part of his core structure in almost all of his tangos, creating a regular conversation between the instruments, one calling and the other responding. Listen to:

Adiós Arrabal (the title gives you advance notice that the song is a Buenos Aires nostalgia trip).
Here the bandoneón calls, the violin answers; then the violin calls and the piano answers; then the voice calls and the bandoneón answers. D'Agostino is part of the exchange throughout, punctuating the conversations with his staccato piano keys.

He has another structural signature sound, created by alternating the lead instrument in his phrases (whilst maintaining the Call and Response conversations). Listen to:

  * *Tres Esquinas* – another nostalgic Buenos Aires lyric. Here the lead instrument passes democratically from the bandoneón, to the violin, to the piano, and then to the voice.

Singers

The singer most closely associated with D'Agostino is Angel Vargas. He was a working class man from the Buenos Aires barrio of Parque Patricios. In 1932, when D'Agostino first recruited him, Vargas was supporting his occasional singing by working as a lathe operator in a food processing factory.

Vargas' singing style commands attention, not by force, but by his gentle recalling of fond memories. This, together with his working class background, made him a local favourite. Mix in the lyrics about the old Buenos Aires, and it is easy to see how the Two Angels came to symbolise Buenos Aires tango in the early 1940s.

The first D'Agostino/Vargas recording was in November 1940 and the last, ninety-four recordings later, in September 1946. During all of these years D'Agostino recorded only seven instrumentals, demonstrating the importance he placed upon his singer Vargas.

Another singer appeared in 1943 - the now little known Raúl Aldao - who recorded three tangos all on one day - the 8th August. Investigations show that D'Agostino recruited Aldao as an emergency measure following a dramatic walkout by Vargas and all of the orchestra musicians. The strike was about pay, and was led by the first violinist Ben Holgado Barrios (see *Musicians)*. Much to the intense anger of his colleagues, after a few months Vargas reneged on his loyalty to the protesters and teamed up again with D'Agostino.

There were a few more singers. After Vargas there was Ricardo Ruiz (formerly with Fresedo). He recorded just one track, the wonderful *Cascabelito*; then in the 1950s came Rubén Cané (a Vargas sound-alike) and Roberto Alvar. But *the* D'Agostino singer was, is, and always will be Angel Vargas.

Musicians

Angel D'Agostino leads the orchestra from his piano. Not unlike Di Sarli he holds each piece together by linking the phrases, at times with Biagi-like sharp punctuation, but with more prominence. D'Agostino is part of the orchestral conversation of calling and responding, and taking his turn to be the lead instrument he can be heard in every recording.

His musicians fall in to three main periods: from the first recording in November 1940 to mid 1943, the year in which Vargas and much of the orchestra went on strike; from the middle of 1943 to the departure of Vargas in September 1946; and finally the late era, from 1951 to 1963. The strike had a major impact on the line-up and music of the orchestra.

<u>November 1940 – mid 1943:</u>
D'Agostino's lead bandoneonist was the talented Alfredo Attadía, who had grown up playing alongside the likes of the young De Angelis and Troilo, and had become part of Biagi's first orchestra in 1939. He was also D'Agostino's musical arranger, and the co-composer of tangos such as *Tres Esquinas* and *El Cocherito*.

The other bandoneonists included Miguel Bonano - who was already a tango legend. He had extensive experience of performing across Europe, including playing for the

King of Spain and, separately, Benito Mussolini. He had played in the orchestras of Donato, Demare, Biagi and many more before he joined D'Agostino.

The lead violinist was Benjamin Holgado Barrios whose violin can be heard 'responding' in *Adiós Arrabal,* and as the lead in the closing minute of *Tres Esquinas.* The other violinists were Vicente Russo and Bernardo Weber. And to complete the strings line-up, the double bass player was Francisco de Lorenzo.

Mid-1943 – September 1946:
The strike was about rates of pay per recording session, and it led to deep, painful division. Violinist Barrios took a leading role in the dispute, which resulted in Vargas and everybody else leaving in the middle of 1943.

The striking musicians started their own orchestra, led by bandoneonist Attadía and Vargas, but their dreams collapsed after only a couple of months when Vargas abandoned them to return to D'Agostino. They each pursued their own professional careers separately and had varying degrees of success (but not within any of our twenty orchestras). Sadly, less than two years after the split from D'Agostino, the violinist Barrios died of cancer at the age of thirty-three.

D'Agostino's re-formed line-up recorded from August 1943 and included as lead bandoneonist, the misleadingly named Eduardo Del Piano. Del Piano can be seen in the 1933 film *'Tango!'*, to the far right of the bandoneón line up in Fresedo's orchestra. He became the arranger of D'Agostino's 'new' orchestra, and the stand-out bandoneón pieces from this period are usually his. Listen to his opening clarion call, resembling the horn of the Buenos Aires tram (which, according to the lyrics, breaks the siesta):

    * *El Cornetín del Tranvía* (1944)

The other musicians during this period already had good tango pedigrees when they arrived, and ably built on their predecessors' slow and smooth style. But then in 1947 the orchestra came to a natural end. As D'Agostino explained, 'these things just happen sometimes'. D'Agostino took a break. Del Piano and Vargas recorded together, but did not achieve the quality or the popular appeal of the D'Agostino years.

1951 to 1963:
The return of D'Agostino to the recording studios in 1951 produced some excellent tracks, including several re-recordings of earlier hits (although they are not heard so often at today's milongas). The most popular numbers from this era include the instrumental *Café Dominguez* (with the speaking voice of Julian Centeya poetically introducing the track), *Esquinas Porteñas* (with singer Rubén Cané), and *Cascabelito* (with singer Ricardo Ruiz). The bandoneonists during this time included Máximo Mori and Santiago Coppola – both former members of Lucio Demare's orchestra.

D'Agostino Summary

- Calm, wistful and nostalgic
- Two Angels partnership with singer Angel Vargas
- Call and Response musical conversations

Alfredo De Angelis

Personal Story

Alfredo De Angelis was born in the outskirts of Buenos Aires in 1912, and enjoyed a childhood that was remarkably blessed tango-wise. His father Virgilio was an artist, pianist, violinist, and bandoneonist and was active in all things creative. His parents' home was often filled with the tango greats of the day, including their relative Samuel Castriota (composer of *Mi Noche Triste*) who used to bring his friends to visit, among them Carlos Gardel and José Razzano.

Because of these early links to the tango world it is of little surprise to discover that the first instrument he learnt to play was the bandoneón (despite it being an infamously difficult instrument for even the most experienced musicians to learn). His gift for music was such that he started to learn the piano at the same time and, by the age of thirteen, had achieved his diploma as a piano teacher.

His early experiences followed a similar track to many of the great tango pianists: he found work playing in a music shop promoting sales of sheet music and records; then he went on to play in a dance school, providing the music for the classes; and then, almost inevitably, he worked in the cinema accompanying the silent films.

By the early 1930s Alfredo had played piano in several famous tango orchestras, and it was during that time that he met and accompanied Carlos Dante (his future singer). Between 1936 and 1938 he teamed up with one of Lomuto's bandoneonists, Daniel Alvarez, to form their own orchestra, but was soon lured away to join the high profile orchestra of Francisco Lauro, where he stayed for two years. During that time he gained the attention of the owner of the Marabú club, who offered him work and helped to supply musicians for him to form his own orchestra. His journey from then on was a fast upward trajectory, with plenty of work in clubs and on popular radio shows, and, starting in July 1943 a (very) long running recording contract. This meteoric rise was helped significantly by the personal patronage of Francisco Canaro.

We can not be sure whose idea it was that De Angelis' father, Virgilo, should become a regular violinist in his son's orchestra. His inclusion may have been based on merit, it could have been due to his son's respect and gratitude, or it could have been to avoid an unbearable paternal sulk. (Perhaps this is yet another side story waiting to be told by somebody?).

From his early boyhood days Alfredo De Angelis had the nickname of 'El Colorado', the red head – an unusual hair colour for Argentinians of Italian descent. Black and white photographs give us no clue to this hallmark feature, but we can appreciate his nickname by watching the colour YouTube video clips from his appearances on the Buenos Aires Crónica TV channel (some of which feature his tango singer daughter, Gigi).

De Angelis was the composer of three of his most popular tangos: *Pregonera*, *Pastora*, and *Remolino*, all recorded with the duets of Carlos Dante and Julio Martel.

Signature Sounds

There are widely varying opinions about the merits of De Angelis music today, much as there were in his heyday. This is because of the feel of his music, the overall signature sound.

In the 1940s he was hugely popular as *the* dance orchestra, and the tango masses all across South America loved his music. He filled the dance halls, enjoyed a fanatically dedicated radio audience, and had substantial record sales. However, commentators described his music as simple and lacking in imagination and innovation. They compared his music to a merry-go-round, partly because the simple phrases that just went around and around, and partly because the sound itself was a little like a funfair Wurlitzer organ. Yet dancers loved the simplicity and the repeated phrases. This obvious appeal to tango feet rather than to the refined tango ear, and the resulting derogatory comments in the face of massive popular appeal, is reminiscent of the split in opinion about D'Arienzo in the mid 1930s.

D'Arienzo has retained his mass appeal, but De Angelis has not. Several of his duets with Dante and Martel are well loved, but generally his repertoire is considered by many to be too flowery and over orchestrated. Michael Lavocah describes De Angelis music as 'light romantic' –

it is so light that the violins feel as though they take off, soaring up to the clouds.

De Angelis' daughter Gigi said that his music was always happy and optimistic, and that the structure was simple (like in the old days), but delivered in a contemporary style. She described his style as nostalgic but not regressive. An example of this approach is in his recording of the Old Guard classic: *Soy Un Arlequin (1945)*. It was composed in 1929 by Discépolo, and excellent earthy versions were recorded in the same year by Canaro, Lomuto, Di Sarli, and even 'pre-D'Arienzo D'Arienzo' with singer Francisco Fiorentino; and also by solo singers Alberto Gómez, Ignacio Corsini and Azucena Maizani (yes, all these tracks were released in the same year!).

In 1945, to underline his nostalgic message, De Angelis purposefully selected another 'old classic' - Carlos Dante - to perform in front of the microphone. Dante's tango pedigree was 'old school'. He started singing for the established tango orchestras back in 1927, so it was a surprise move for De Angelis to bring him out of tango retirement. Their recording of *Soy Un Arlequin* starts conventionally enough as Dante enters in his inimitable grounded style. But after one minute there are high violin accompaniments (pure De Angelis) that continue through to the final part, when the full-blown bandoneón merry-go-round kicks in. This version of *Soy*

Un Arlequin is no longer the Old Guard classic – it is a De Angelis special.

His typical soaring violins can also be heard in *La Vida Me Engañó* (1946), which makes instructive listening when compared to Di Sarli's version recorded four months later, with its much more restrained violins.

Prolonged vocal endings also provide a frequent contribution to the De Angelis signature sound. Listen to the ends of the duets with Carlos Dante and Julio Martel:
* *Pregonera* (1945); *Remolino* (1946); *Pastora* (1948).
These drawn out endings were not restricted to duets but occasionally are to be heard with solo singers. Listen to:

  * *Mi Novia de Ayer* (1944) with singer Floreal Ruiz;
  * *Jirón Porteño* (1946) with singer Julio Martel;
  * *Mocosita* (1949) with singer Carlos Dante.

Singers

Floreal Ruiz first recorded with De Angelis in July 1943. A year later he was recruited by Aníbal Troilo (see *Singers* in the Troilo chapter for more). Floreal's biographer describes him as having the most natural, effortless singing manner, as if talking intimately from an armchair. Listen to:

* *Bajo El Cono Azul* (1944).

De Angelis is often described on tango websites as the promoter of 1940s duets, a title that somewhat overplays the extent of his innovation. Although it is true to say that De Angelis used duets to great effect, and that those recordings are still amongst the most popular enjoyed today, tango duets had been successfully used throughout the 1930s (for example by Canaro and Lomuto) and in the early 1940s (by Donato and Troilo, amongst others).

His most successful duo combination was the pairing of old timer Carlos Dante (who had been singing since the late 1920s with the likes of D'Arienzo, Caló and Canaro) and newcomer Julio Martel. Their first duet for De Angelis was in August 1944, *Sonar y Nada Más,* but this simply followed the proven duet formula released the previous year by Canaro (Adrián and Roldán) and by Troilo (Fiorentino and Marino).

However, when he got into his stride De Angelis was the most prolific and successful user of duets in the tango dance market from 1944 to 1945. This was with the combination of Dante and Martel, and then, up to the early 1950s, with Dante and Oscar Larroca.

It may be an unkind thought, but it could be said that De Angelis relied upon two voices to provide what was lacking in his instruments - the intricate interplay of melody lines. His instrumentals in the 1940s are noticeably weaker than the vocal numbers. However, he did produce some rousing instrumentals in the late 1950s with *Pavadita, Tango Club*, and *Mi Dolor*.

Although he was not a singer, the vocal contribution of the glosador (announcer) Néstor Rodi must be acknowledged. He poetically builds the mood and anticipation of several of the De Angelis popular dance recordings (although they are often edited out by DJs when played at milongas). Listen to the (unedited) openings of:
    * *Buenos Aires de Ayer* (1943);
    * *De Igual a Igual* (1944).

Musicians

Alfredo's daughter published *Alfredo de Angelis, El Fenomeno Social,* in which she explains that her father, in a similar way to Osvaldo Pugliese, operated his orchestra as a co-operative, with each musician receiving equal pay. In that way there were no individual stars and no internal rivalries. This approach is reflected in his music – there are few featured solos.

Alfredo De Angelis himself was the pianist and, as such, is to be heard on every recording. Two opened packets of cigarettes always sat upon his piano, supplying part of his eighty-a-day habit – a habit that may have contributed to his failing lungs in later years.

His lead violinist, responsible for the soaring strings, was Wenceslao Cinosi, ably supported by colleagues Angel Raúl Vilar, Alberto Cicero and Hipólito Caron. The famous merry-go-round bandoneonists included Carlos Cubría, Eduardo Talián, Guillermo Vilar and Alfredo Dafuncio. To complete the picture, the double bass player was Hugo Besnatti.

De Angelis Summary

- Red headed pianist
- Whirling orchestration with soaring violins
- Duets

PART FOUR:
THE COMPLEX

Julio De Caro

Personal Story

The reasons for including the De Caro orchestra are similar to the reasons for including Roberto Firpo - both were immensely influential and popular in their time, and yet, regrettably, neither is heard very much at today's milongas. Such was the influence of the De Caro orchestra that there may not have been any 'Complex' orchestras without it. Laurenz, Pugliese and Troilo would certainly not have sounded as they do.

Why do we not hear much of De Caro? Because the music was arranged primarily for the 'refined' ear rather than the dancer. The orchestra wanted to show the world that tango could also be 'proper' music, as good as European Classical.

Although the orchestra is commonly known by the name of Julio De Caro, I prefer to call it more inclusively the 'De Caro Orchestra', because the De Caro phenomenon is as much attributable to his brother Francisco as to Julio himself.

The De Caro family was torn apart by the conflict between tango and classical music. The father, Don José De Caro, had been Director of the Music Academy at the world famous Teatro alla Scala in Milan. He had trained his children in the beauty of classical music, and had plans for his sons' virtuoso careers. All of that exposure and training gave the two eldest sons, Francisco and Julio, the foundation for the sound that they would produce in another world. The collision of cultures in the De Caro household came in 1917 when the eighteen year old Julio defied his father once too often, using his sacred violin to perform common tangos in the company of the likes of the tango pioneers Roberto Firpo, Eduardo Arolas and Vicente Greco. His father banished him from the family home. Shortly afterwards, Francisco abandoned the family home too, in order to commit his life to tango. The domestic trauma only became worse when three remaining younger sons Emilio, Alberto and José also followed the tango path. Father and sons were not reconciled for decades.

By December 1923 Francisco De Caro had formed a quartet – with himself on piano, his brother Emilo on violin, plus the star bandoneonists Pedro Maffia and Luis Petrucelli. Julio had recently become unemployed (as the orchestra he was in had just broken up), and so Francisco invited him to join. The well-connected Julio soon secured a prestigious performing contract for the band, but had told the impresario that the name of the orchestra was the Julio De Caro Sexteto. When Julio broke the news to his colleagues (including his brother), the change of name caused some considerable furore, but the lucrative contract saved the day. They added the renowned bass player Leopoldo Thompson and the sextet were soon performing for the great and the good of Argentina. By early 1924 they were recording.

Luis Petrucelli left that same year and his place was taken by the young Pedro Laurenz. The following year, the gifted bassist Thompson died suddenly, aged thirty-five. Maffia left in the same year, enabling Laurenz to take the position of first bandoneonist (it was from here that the Laurenz story starts – see the next chapter).

In the early 1930s the orchestra developed a fuller symphonic sound, with more complex arrangements in order to, in Julio's own words, 'ennoble the tango'. They had many supporters and influenced many of the later maestros, but public interest in their music was waning. In 1934 all of the musicians abandoned the De Caro brothers, and within two years they were hit with another setback – the unexpected popularity of Juan D'Arienzo's thumping simplicity, the antithesis of the De Caro style.

In an attempt to redefine themselves in 1936 the De Caros formed two groups - Los Virtuosos Quintet (as a result of a competition to find the top tango virtuoso musicians) and the Orquesta Melodica Internacional. The former had the benefit of Elvino Vardaro's violin and Ciriaco Ortiz's bandoneón, and the latter had Cayetano Puglisi – all immensely talented and influential tango musicians.

A study of De Caro's recording history reflects that after the mid 1930s the orchestra had a dwindling impact in the world of popular tango, particularly following the post-D'Arienzo boom in tango dance music. In the late 1920s they recorded about thirty tracks per year, culminating in a triumphant ninety tracks in 1930 (having changed recording company to Brunswick). But after 1938 their output had reduced to about ten per year, winding down to just two tracks in 1944.

It is at this point that long-time admirer Osvaldo Pugliese stepped in to show his respect to the De Caros. They were the first to record the Pugliese composition *Recuerdo*, as early as 1926, and so as soon as Pugliese secured his own recording contract he repaid the compliment by including Julio's composition *Mala Junta* on his second record in August 1943. And to deliberately keep the De Caro sound in the public's ears over the next few years, he released the De Caro classics *Tierra Querida*, *Mala Pinta*, *El Monito* and *Boedo*.

The De Caro Orchestra re-emerged between 1949 and 1953, re-recording several of their earlier sextet hits. Understandably the recording quality is better than the late 1920s tracks, and so it is the later versions that tend to be played at milongas, if they are played at all.

Signature Sounds

Knowing the family story, it becomes clear that the overall De Caro sound is a homage to the classical roots of their father. Even from the early sextet years of 1926 to 1929, the complex arrangements stand out from the music of their peers - Canaro, Firpo, OTV, and even Fresedo. Their musical message is to increase wider appreciation that 'tango is music too' –a quote attributed to Julio De Caro, no doubt as a prolonged and pained plea to his father that he did not forsake his classical training when he followed the path of tango.

Although the music is complex and intelligently constructed, it is neither formal nor dull. On the contrary, it is often surprisingly playful. From 1926 to the 1940s many of the tracks include whistling, the comical use of the musical saw, fireworks and popping corks, with members of the orchestra shouting or making unusual noises. Listen to:

* *Vayan Saliendo* (1928);
* *Tierra Negra* (1940).

By the 1950s the overall sound was still familiarly De Caro but without the musical jokes – perhaps the brothers were getting too old for all of that? Listen to:

* *Tierra Querida* (1952)

One of their many experimental phases included the Orquesta Melodica Internacional in 1936, which had amongst its instruments brass, woodwind and percussion. We can hear all of those together in the milonga hit:

  * *De Contrapunto* (1936)

However, the new sound attracted increasing criticism from the old fans, forcing the orchestra to return to its former, more traditional style in 1939.

The recordings from 1949 to 1953 have a similar feel and construction to those in the late 1920s, but they sound fuller, as they are played by an orchestra rather than a sextet, and the recording quality is much better.

Singers

Much of De Caro's discography is instrumental, which is consistent with the De Caro style of aligning tango music to the more classical genre. When vocals are added it is a surprise that the singers are not among the most sophisticated, in order to suit the more genteel tastes of the De Caro target audiences. Perhaps they were chosen to demonstrate the avant-garde mix of 'proper' music and the more coarse street tango.

This mix seemed to suit the sound of the 1920s to early 1930s, particularly with the inclusion of the 'Old Guard' regulars Luis Díaz (who also sang with Donato and OTV) and Teófilo Ibáñez (also heard with Donato, OTV, Fresedo and Firpo). As the music progressed into the late 1930s and early 1940s, the De Caros did not follow the trend of using more mature tango voices (such as Podestá, Fiorentino and Vargas).

Listen to the 1927 and 1949 instrumental versions of Julio De Caro's composition *Copacabana*, both so sweet and melodic, and then listen to the 1941 version with singer Héctor Farrell. The music remains tender, but the voice is less so and sounds more appropriate to the feel of the 1920s.

The other De Caro singers in this era included Agustín Volpe and Carlos Vivan but is not until the end of the De

Caro recording history that we see some movement in choice of singer. Listen to:

* *Mi Dolor* (1950) with singer Orlando Verri;

Esta Noche de Luna (1951) with Roberto Medina. Their voices fit well, and it is a shame that they did not get the chance to get in to full flow before the De Caro brothers retired in 1953.

Musicians

In the recording years from 1924 to 1930 the core of the musicians were, of course, the De Caro brothers. Francisco was not only the founder of the orchestra and a talented pianist, but a composer and arranger too. His style influenced many later pianists - Lucio Demare said that he tried to model himself on Francisco De Caro.

Julio is the violinist, and there are many photographs that show him using a Stroh violin (a violin with an amplifying horn) to gain improved directional sound projection. He was supported in the violin section by his brother Emilio.

Once the lead bandoneonist Pedro Maffia departed in 1926, Pedro Laurenz took his seat and brought in his friend Armando Blasco to become his second. They stayed until 1934, and all of the bandoneón decorations you can hear during those years are from their dextrous fingers. Listen to:

* *El Taita (Raza Criollo)* 1928

In this Francisco De Caro keeps the beat on piano and gives himself a short solo, it is probably Emilo De Caro playing pizzicato violin over the masterful Pedro Laurenz on bandoneón, followed by a typical Julio De Caro horn violin lead.

From 1934 onwards the replacement lead bandoneonist was Carlos Marcucci, who is prominent in most, if not all, of the recordings until he left in 1950.

De Caro Summary

- Dramatic family split - classical versus tango
- Tango aimed at the discerning ear
- Contrasts with elements of the street – whistles, crowd noises and rough voices

Pedro Laurenz

Personal Story

Pedro Laurenz was born Pedro Blanco Acosta in Buenos Aires in 1902, the son of Pedro Blanco and Rafaela Acosta, and as a young boy he learnt to play the violin. Aged only fourteen his life dramatically changed when his father died and his mother took him (and his older sister Lila) to live in Montevideo, Uruguay. There he met for the first time his two older half-brothers, Eustaquio and Félix Laurenz, the sons of his mother and her first husband (who had been a Uruguayan bandoneonist).

Eustaquio and Félix were professional bandoneón players themselves, and encouraged their half-brother's musical prowess. They convinced him that he should try the bandoneón rather than the violin. Both taught him the rudiments of this difficult instrument, a long and patient labour of love, particularly as, at that time, Pedro could not read a musical score.

By the time he was twenty, in 1922, he had played alongside Eustaquio in a Montevideo tango orchestra, with the young violinists Edgardo Donato and Roberto Zerillo, and not long afterwards he left for Buenos Aires.

Once there he was regularly playing, meeting and joining with other musicians, performing on the radio and in central Buenos Aires venues.

In 1925 the successful De Caro Sextet was looking to replace the bandoneonist Luis Petrucelli. The De Caro brothers were pointed towards Pedro Blanco Acosta, who secured the deal by using his family connection to Eustaquio and Félix, both of whom Julio De Caro knew from his time in Montevideo. It was De Caro who gave Pedro the name by which he would forever be known, saying 'I baptise you Pedro Laurenz'.

The arrival of the unknown musician in the De Caro line up was viewed suspiciously by lead bandoneonist Pedro Maffia, but as soon as Laurenz got in to his stride playing in their first tango together, Maffia smiled and the two worked superbly together thereafter. To differentiate between the two Pedros in the orchestra, the younger Laurenz was always called Pedrito. Those years were the foundations of Laurenz's future style.

In 1934 he led a departure of musicians from the De Caro orchestra to form his own, for which he also recruited pianist Osvaldo Pugliese. The sound was avant-garde, building on the De Caro style, and appealed to a particular audience, one that was intellectually attracted to complex music and virtuoso playing.

To achieve commercial success timing is everything, and the Laurenz orchestra's first years on the tango scene overlapped with the 1935/36 explosion of the D'Arienzo sound – the complete antithesis of his De Caro style complexity. The recording companies, probably quite correctly, did not see the commercial viability of his complex sound and so it was not until 1937 that Laurenz managed to secure a recording contract. That contract proved to be an extremely limited arrangement. He recorded only four tracks (two tangos, a milonga, and a ranchera), and only another two the following year!

His most popular time came in the early and mid 1940s, helped considerably by his choice of singers, more of which shortly.

Laurenz was an accomplished composer, and from the earliest days with De Caro they worked together to write *Mala Junta* and *Orgullo Criollo* (each recorded by De Caro in 1927/28 and by Laurenz in the 1940s). He composed the frequently played *Milonga de Mis Amores*, recording two versions: one in 1937 with his singer Héctor Farrel, and seven years later in 1944 as an instrumental. The milonga was also recorded by Canaro (1937) and by D'Arienzo (1970).

Signature Sounds

1937 was the time of D'Arienzo's stomping raw tangos, and others were following his style. In contrast, Canaro with singer Maida, and Fresedo with singer Ray, were staying with the gentle symphonic sound mainly aimed at the sit-down-and-listen cabaret audiences. As for Laurenz, he was ahead of his time - the equivalent of Jimi Hendrix and his guitar in the 1960s. He was not as well known as many of the other orchestras because he was not commercially successful, being regarded as too avant-garde, too adventurous.

In comparison to what else was happening in 1937 his music is surprisingly complex but, unlike De Caro, he brought the complex successfully to the dance floor. The centrepiece of the music at that stage was Laurenz himself on bandoneón.

His creativity was to be a great influence on two other orchestra leaders – Osvaldo Pugliese and Aníbal Troilo. Listen to:

 * *Arrabal* (1937)

There is not only energy and complexity in this track but also a change of flow in the music. At points, for example at about thirty seconds, the flow starts to recede, resuming at about forty seconds. This ebb-and-flow effect is one that we do not hear for another five years or so, when it was exploited by Pugliese. Also in Laurenz's

Arrabal you will hear a new sound of syncopated phrases, particularly after two minutes. A similar rhythm can be heard in Troilo's *Comme Il Faut* (1938) and *Milongueando en el Cuarenta* (1941).

Tango authors Michael Lavocah and Christian Tobler say respectively that: Laurenz sounds like an out of control train just managing to stay on the tracks allowing relief only when he finally manages to pull safely in to the station; and that he creates a musical volcano, internally close to the point of explosion but externally solid and controlled. Listen again to the end part of *Arrabal* and enjoy this imagery.

Singers

Laurenz's first recording was made in 1937, with a singer recruited the year before (Héctor Cardinale) although, for some reason, Laurenz insisted that he changed his name to Héctor Farrel. Renaming singers seemed to be the prerogative of orchestra leaders, perhaps as a way of asserting their authority. The recording was an unusual choice. Laurenz is the only one of our twenty orchestras to launch his recording career with a milonga. *Milonga de Mis Amores* was Laurenz's own composition, and one that is frequently played and danced today. Farrel gets a mere twenty seconds to sing in the closing minute, but in his next, and final recording with Laurenz (the tango *Abandono* composed by Laurenz's mentor Pedro Maffia), he gets a bit more time to exercise his vocal chords.

Juan Carlos Casas arrived in 1938 and left in 1942. He recorded fifteen tracks, including two milongas, *Milonga Compadre (*1938) and *Chatero de Aquel Entonces* (1942), which still keep the dance floors busy today. Meanwhile Laurenz kept experimenting with his singers. The singers during this period were Martin Podestá (no relation to Alberto, as in both cases their surnames were stage names), Alberto Del Campo and Alberto Fuentes. At the time there was little public acclaim for any of them, although the recordings are regularly played and danced today.

In 1943 Laurenz pulled off a significant coup, securing Alberto Podestá from Carlos Di Sarli. Podestá recorded sixteen tracks in 1943 and 1944 and became the most popular of Laurenz's singers. Listen to his velvet voice:

* *Nunca Tuvo Novio* (1943)

After Alberto Podestá two new singers arrived in 1944, Carlos Bermúdez and Jorge Linares, each of them recording individually, and once together as a duet. Listen to the lovely vals:

* *Mendocina* (1944)

In 1946 Laurenz recorded two unremarkable tracks with singer Héctor Juncal followed by a long recording gap until 1952/53, when he returned with, the now little heard, Alfredo Del Rio.

Musicians

Pedro Laurenz himself was responsible for the virtuoso playing of the bandoneón, clearly heard on many of his recordings. From the orchestra formation in 1934 and its first recordings in 1937 he was supported by his bandoneonist friend from the De Caro orchestra, Armando Blasco. Blasco left in 1939 and was replaced by Angel Dominguez. Also on bandoneón was Rolando Gavioli, the brother of Donato's singer Romeo.

Laurenz's violinists included Mauricio Mise, a tango composer whose work included *Tu Confidencia* (recorded in 1942 by Donato with Romeo Gavioli) and *Si No Me Enganas Corazón* (recorded in 1939 by Fresedo with Ruiz and in 1956 by De Angelis with Dante).

His double bass player throughout was Alberto Celenza, who also played violin and bandoneón, and was a composer of tangos, including *No Me Extraña* (recorded in 1940 by Laurenz with Casas).

Also working with Laurenz over the long-term was Héctor Grané, a tango composer whose work included *Esta Noche Al Pasar* (recorded by Laurenz with Casas in 1944, and Tanturi with Campos the year after) and *Soy Aquel Viajero* (recorded by Di Sarli in 1947).

Laurenz Summary

- Jimi Hendrix of the bandoneón world
- Ahead of his time, not commercially successful
- Influenced Pugliese and Troilo

Osvaldo Pugliese

Personal Story

Osvaldo Pugliese remains revered by his fans, who refer to him to as San (Saint) Pugliese. He is loved for his mastery and development of the tango genre, and for his consistent benevolence and humility.

He was born in 1905 in Buenos Aires. His father, a passionate, well-connected amateur tango flautist, taught Osvaldo the flute and introduced him to many influential figures in the tango music scene.

From the age of fifteen Osvaldo Pugliese was playing piano in many tango quartets, quintets, and sextets. Later he played with Roberto Firpo, Pedro Maffia, Pedro Laurenz and Miguel Caló, among others. He also formed his own bands, one of which was with Alfredo Gobbi, and the young bandoneonist Aníbal Troilo.

Pugliese's experience with these orchestras allowed him to experiment not just with music but also with the application of his communist principles to the working practices of the orchestras. He operated his various bands as co-operatives, meaning that all members of the orchestra had equal say in the organisation and in the musical output, and were paid according to their input. He said *'We all participate and we all put in our grain of sand...we all have the same opportunity, everyone from top to bottom'*.

Pugliese held strong views on equal rights and individual freedom at a time when Argentina was generally under the control of authoritarian regimes. He was a prominent member of the Communist Party and had built up a loyal following from members of the Party. This brought him under close scrutiny by the national security authorities, and he was frequently detained. He regarded 1948 as the year when the authorities nearly finished him off completely, not only by arresting him, but also by constantly harassing his musicians, the venue organisers and the audiences. During his many incarcerations his supporters would lobby the Government to release him, and his orchestra would place a red carnation on his piano during performances – their absent leader forever in their hearts.

Pugliese remained true to his social and political ideas throughout his life, and was bravely vocal in his criticisms of the military dictatorships during the horrors of the 1960s and 1970s. Soon after the return of democracy, aged eighty years old, he achieved a personal dream - to take the people's tango to the centre of high culture in Buenos Aires, the Teatro Colon.

Pugliese was a prolific composer of tangos, many of them becoming his most iconic recordings. He composed the famous piece *Recuerdo* (1944) as a teenager, and re-recorded it several times right through to the 1980s. Many others recorded it too, including Troilo, Tanturi, Lomuto, and OTV. His other notable compositions include *La Yumba* (1946), *Negracha* (1948), and *Malandraca* (1949).

Signature Sounds

The Pugliese sound is most closely associated with his onomatopoeic *La Yumba*. It is only onomatopoeic of course if pronounced with a Buenos Aires porteño accent, *zhoóm-ba*. The sound is said to be like that of the steam driven hammers in an iron foundry – a release of steam and a thud. Reportedly the bandoneonists would raise their bent legs upon which their instruments rested and bring their feet crashing down to the floor to emphasis the *'-ba'*. Listen to:

   * *La Yumba* (1946).

As well as the commonly heard 'yumba' effect, the overall characteristic of Pugliese's music is one of complex contrasts in the pace of the tango, or as tango historian Luis Sierra puts it, he 'weaves a very fine polyrhythmic network'. For example *La Yumba* begins with the core rhythm then changes at about fifteen seconds, the pattern repeats until a new rhythmic pattern enters just after the one minute mark, then a further new rhythm begins twenty-five seconds later. 'Woven together' is the right term. It is complex, but not chaotic.

The music flows from the driving, irresistibly powerful 'yumba' rhythm in to a chasm where the dancing beat is lost, almost silent. As the listener, and particularly the dancer, wonders what will happen next, one of the instruments will pick itself up again, dust itself down and head off in a different direction. Although this construction can be difficult to dance to, the contrasts build into a carefully constructed story. Dancing to Pugliese is like dancing to a cryptic crossword! Listen to:

 * *Derecho Viejo* (1945)

This track is not an extreme instance of complex contrasts, but it has many elements of the Pugliese style. The tango is well known and there are versions by almost every other orchestra – but none of them is like this.

The second half of the 1940s saw Pugliese take the dancehalls by storm. His recordings reveal an intensity of emotion that exceeds anything being produced by his peers (including Troilo and Laurenz). Listen to:

 * *Amurado* (1944)

Pugliese's later work in the 1950s includes big potent numbers with powerful singers, almost operatic in their delivery, which leave you feeling emotionally drained and/or elated! These are not the sort of tangos you can dance just because they happen to be playing – you and your partner have to be ready for them. Listen to:

 * *Remembranza* (1956)

Singers

Pugliese's first recording, in July 1943, has become one of his most popular tracks with a singer - *Farol* with Roberto Chanel (real name Alfredo Mazzochi who took his stage name from the fashionable perfume). His voice apparently had the dominant sounds of a man from the streets of Buenos Aires – characteristics that are not easily recognisable for those of us who are not native to that city.

Chanel stayed with Pugliese until 1947, recording thirty-one tracks, including three duets with Alberto Morán. Chanel left to sing with other orchestras, and later followed a solo career, but did not achieve the same popularity. After suffering several illnesses he died aged only fifty-eight years old. Listen to:

   * *Farol* (1943)

In 1945 Pugliese recruited Alberto Morán. Whilst praising all of his singers over the decades, Pugliese said that Chanel and Morán were the two that integrated best of all, in as much as that they were like another instrument in the orchestra, rather than out-in-front singers.

Morán was different to Chanel in that he had more emotion and drama in his voice and, as it turned out, a powerful sensuality on stage that had a phenomenal effect on his numerous female fans. He recorded just over fifty tracks, including duets, until he left in 1954. Listen to him in:

   * *Una Vez* (1946)

From 1945 onwards Pugliese tried to retain at least two singers so that his releases offered vocal variety. His records often featured one singer on the A side and another on the B side, and so after Chanel departed Pugliese needed another singer to contrast with Morán. He looked for a similar style to Chanel, and he found it in Jorge Vidal – a hard living street singer with a tough reputation. Vidal revealed a fascinating glimpse in to Buenos Aires street life in the 1930s and 1940s to the tango historian Néstor Pinsón, including a description of an incident when his mother threw herself in front of the President's car in order to highlight her impoverished plight.

Pugliese's use of the street voice was not only artistically driven but also politically ideological. He wanted his tango to symbolise the working man.

Vidal was a restless man who stayed just over a year and left only eight recordings. His last one seems to bring out his rough street character best of all. Listen to:

   * *Un Baile de Beneficio* (1950)

Vidal's departure left Morán alone for two years, apart from a period in 1953 and 1954, when Pugliese also used Juan Carlos Cobos, until both singers left. From 1954 to 1958 came Miguel Montero and Jorge Maciel (who stayed on until the late 1960s). Maciel had made his name singing with the orchestra of Alfredo Gobbi, but is better known now as the dramatic singer of Pugliese - dramatic because he wrings out every emotion from the dancer in the likes of:

* *Cascabelito* (1955)

The idea of contrast always appealed to Pugliese, continuing in to the early 1960s with the pairing of the tender voiced Maciel with the tough, often harsh, tones of Alfredo Belusi.

His later singers take us beyond the era of danceable recordings, although it would be remiss not to acknowledge the hugely popular Abel Córdoba. Córdoba recorded with Pugliese for over twenty-three years (from 1963 to 1986), and stayed with him even longer, right up to Pugliese's final performances.

Musicians

Osvaldo Pugliese directed his orchestra from the piano and so the piano work on nearly all of his recordings, from 1943 through to 1986, is his own.

His relationship with his musicians was extraordinary and engendered tremendous loyalty in both directions. The majority of his musicians stayed with him for a period of nearly thirty years. This core group was as responsible for the Pugliese sound as Osvaldo himself, whose particular talent was to make it all come together. He created a nurturing environment where his musicians could grow, develop, and contribute.

Let us start not with the usual bandoneóns nor violins but with the often unsung hero of the *orquesta típica* – the bass player. They are all too often omitted from the annals of tango history, and generally overlooked by tango aficionados, yet all of these twenty orchestras were blessed with skilful bass players. It is an instrument that was essential to the sound, the rhythm and the mood of the performances, and some of the players had more influence than their musical contribution alone - one such outstanding player was Aniceto Rossi.

Rossi was born in 1898. The son and brother of bass players, he was a mentor and stable influence to many of the younger musicians, and a confidante to Pugliese. Such was his musical prowess, and his standing within the orchestra, that in 1949 Pugliese gave him an extended solo in his recording of *Canaro in Paris* – a rare honour afforded to a tango bass player. The following year, in 1950, Pugliese recorded a composition by his bandoneonist Esteban Gilardi titled *Don Aniceto*, dedicated to Rossi. When Aniceto retired in 1960 his place was taken by his son Alcides Rossi – a third generation bass player.

Pugliese's lead bandoneonist was Osvaldo Ruggiero who joined aged seventeen (several years before the first recording contract) and stayed until the mid 1950s. He provided Pugliese with several compositions including *N.N.* and *Yunta de Oro*. The other regular bandoneonists between 1943 and the mid 1950s were Esteban Gilardi, Jorge Caldera (from 1945), and Oscar Castagniaro (from 1944). The regular violinists during that same period were Enrique Camerano, Julio Carrasco, Oscar Herrero and Jaime Tursky (replaced in 1948 by Emilio Balcarce).

Pugliese Summary

- San (Saint) Pugliese, principled egalitarian
- Dramatic changes of tempo and power

Aníbal Troilo

Personal Story

Aníbal Troilo was born in Buenos Aires on 11th July 1914 – a date subsequently commemorated in Argentina as National Bandoneón Day in his honour. He was the third child of father Aníbal Carmelo Troilo, a retail butcher, and mother Felisa Bagnolo. When his father died Felisa was left to bring up Aníbal and his older brother Marcos (her first born, a daughter, had died young). She struggled to do so, on her meagre income as a street cigarette seller.

The young Aníbal had two passions. One was football (he played regularly for two teams) and the other was the bandoneón. He recalls that he used to spend hours playing a feather pillow as if it were a bandoneón – an early version of the 'air guitar'. He had been mesmerised by the bandoneóns that he heard being played in the cafes around his home. He had a particular vivid memory of being nine years old and seeing a quintet of three guitarists and two bandoneonists in the park. When they had a break, Aníbal took his chance to grab one of the bandoneóns and place it across his knee. Despite their poverty, the next year Aníbal's mother bought him a bandoneón for his tenth birthday. It is a well-known story that she bought it on credit and was paying in monthly instalments, but shortly afterwards the seller disappeared, leaving the Troilo family with a bargain bandoneón. Aníbal kept that bandoneón for the rest of his life.

In the year of his father's death the twelve year-old Aníbal took flowers from the patio at home and placed them on his grave, making a vow that he would learn how to play the bandoneón properly. One year later he was earning a few pesos by accompanying a trio of lady musicians at a cafe in central Buenos Aires. Meanwhile he continued to take lessons from talented musicians, including the maestro Pedro Maffia. He was moving in the right circles and playing in the right style and managed to catch the eye and the ear of the established tango stars of the time. As early as 1933, at the age of nineteen, he appeared playing his bandoneón in a film 'Los Tres Berretines' whilst Luis Díaz sang Araca La Cana. He also played alongside such stars as Julio de Caro, Pedro Laurenz, Angel D'Agostino, Juan D'Arienzo, Juan Carlos Cobián, Ciriaco Ortiz, Elvino Vardaro, Alfredo Gobbi and Osvaldo Pugliese. He formed his own orchestra in 1937, aged only twenty-three.

However, as he came late to the age of tango dance music the vast majority of his long recording life (from 1938 to 1971) is beyond the main dance era. It is, therefore, even more frustrating that his early recording opportunities were cynically curtailed by his first recording company Odeon. As mentioned in the Tanturi chapter, Odeon had a strategy of limiting the output of young rising stars. Odeon signed this young promising orchestra leader and allowed him to make one record in March 1938, *Comme Il Faut* on one side and *Tinta Verde* on the other, and then no more. As he was contracted to them, there was recording silence until three long years later, in March 1941, when he became free to sign with Victor.

The following four years make up the main period of the music that we hear and dance to at milongas, peaking in 1941 to 1943 and with diminishing danceability (for some tastes) from 1944.

We can see Troilo playing, and briefly acting, at many points, in the 1948 film '*El Tango Vuelve a Paris*', most frequently accompanying the singer Alberto Castillo (but there is a short close up of him playing his bandoneón just before the sixteenth minute).

Between 1938 and 1971 Troilo composed over forty tangos, thirteen milongas, six valses, and one habanera, most of which fall into the post-dance style.

Signature Sounds

Astor Piazzolla, (musician, composer, arranger, and friend of Troilo) said that the early designers of the Troilo orchestra sound were the pianist Orlando Goñi and the bass player Kicho Díaz. They took Troilo's natural inclination for the type of complexity that De Caro, Pugliese, and Laurenz favoured, and helped him create an energy-charged D'Arienzo-esque dance orchestra. Listen to:

   * *Comme Il Faut* (1938);
   * *El Tamango* (1941).

Of all of our twenty orchestras it is Troilo's that can be the most troubesome when trying to describe a distinct signature sound. A common feature is that Troilo often contrasts staccato with legato (sharp with smooth) – although others also use this technique, for example Miguel Caló. Meanwhile, some tracks are aggressively rhythmic like D'Arienzo or Tanturi. Then there is the punctuating piano that could sound like either of these, or even Biagi.

Sometimes when trying to identify an orchestra it is necessary to do so by elimination, and this often works best with Troilo. One can quickly dispose of Canaro/Lomuto (there are no clarinets, trumpets, nor cymbals); it is not D'Arienzo (because there is no low violin); Goñi's playing is not discrete enough to be Di

Sarli, nor relentlessly agitated and off the beat to be Biagi; it is not Fresedo (as there is no harp); nor Pugliese because the timing is too regular. Then it is probably Troilo!

However, there somehow *is* something distinct about Troilo's sound. It is just that it is better heard than described in words. Listen to:

   * Milongueando En El Cuarenta (1941)

This instrumental incorporates the style and character of Troilo's best dance music. There is the run of notes like a slow strum on a guitar, the syncopation, and the staccato to legato and back again. In this track each instrument (except Goñi on piano and Fiorentino on vocals) comes to the fore. Listen to the bass player Kicho Díaz supporting both his brother David's violin and, later, Troilo's bandoneón. Listen to the whole, listen to the structure, and then listen again to each of the instruments in turn. This is the sound of Troilo for the dance floor.

To appreciate the style and mastery of both Goñi's piano and Fiorentino's voice we can listen in the same way to:

   * En Esta Tarde Gris (1941)

The same Troilo style and structure is there, with each of the instruments playing their unmistakeable part but, to me, this track is all about piano and vocals.

Singers

Francisco Fiorentino is one of the very few leading singers who retained the name given to him at birth! In 1928 he started off as a bandoneón player for Canaro, Firpo, and D'Arienzo, then discovered that he could sing – initially as the estribillista (chorus singer) for Canaro. However, he was not regarded as a great singer. When he sang with OTV, his voice sounded pedestrian and nasal. Listen to:

Organito Callajero (1931)

A decade later, in March 1941, Troilo started to bring out the best in him. Like D'Agostino/Vargas and Biagi/Ortiz, his name became completely inseparable from his orchestra leader. Troilo/Fiorentino is a combination embedded in many tango fans' minds. Although he lacked power and clarity in his diction, when weaved in to Troilo's music his voice seemed perfect. Listen to:

* *No Te Apures, Cara Blanca* (1942)

He split from Troilo in 1944, having produced some sixty recordings. He went on for a further ten years singing with other respected orchestras, although he never reached the same standards nor achieved the same levels of acclaim.

In 1955 Fiorentino happily told a journalist that the best thing that he could ever imagine was soon to happen -

after his next tour to Mendoza he was going to record with Troilo again. 'Isn't that marvellous?' he said. Sadly, it was not to be. A few months later, returning from his tour, he was involved as a passenger in a car crash, and drowned in a couple of inches of water in a roadside ditch. He was fifty-five. This may be a good time to pause and listen to a few more of the outstanding Troilo and Fiorentino tangos such as *Cada Día Te Extraño Más*, *El Cuarteador*, *Toda Mi Vida*.

Troilo's next singer was Italian-born Alberto Marino. In 1943 he had agreed to sing for Rodolfo Biagi, but Troilo made him a better offer. Marino is described as having a luxurious tenor voice, with more depth of expression than Fiorentino. Listen to:

  * *Tal Vez Sera Tu Voz* (1943)

It was at the recommendation of Marino that Floreal Ruiz joined Troilo in 1944. Ruiz was born in the barrio of Flores. His father, a political anarchist, threw him out of the house, calling him a pimp for wanting to be a singer – although he later forgave him when he heard him sing in 1942. Between 1944 and 1948 Ruiz made over thirty recordings with Troilo. Listen to:

  * *Yuyo Verde* (1945)

In 1947 came Edmundo Rivero, a magnificent bass singer, and later the much loved Roberto Goyeneche, but by this time the Troilo's musical arrangement was less for the dancer's feet and more for the listener's ears.

Musicians

Troilo was a renowned bandoneón player famed for minimalistic and soulful playing. His signature playing, however, is most evident in the later, non-dance years. In fact the later the decade, the more prominent is his bandoneón. During the recording period 1938 to 1944, his individual contribution is much less clear. This was because he was ably accompanied not just by fellow bandoneonists Toto Rodríguez and Eduardo Marino, but for much of the time by the talented Astor Piazzolla. His elder brother Marcos Troilo also joined the bandoneon line up.

Astor Piazzolla was in Troilo's orchestra from 1939 to 1944, the main era of Troilo's music played at today's milongas. As an arranger, Piazzolla was far too elaborate for his leader's tastes. Troilo (who was admired for being able to manage silences in music) would famously take an eraser to the notes and rub out large portions of them. It might be sacrilege, but it is not entirely fanciful, to suggest that Troilo's motives may have been because he was not quite up to playing such dexterous parts on the bandoneón. He was a talented player, but rapid Laurenz-style fingering was not his style.

The key violinist was the admirably loyal David Díaz who joined right at the start in 1938, and stayed some thirty-seven years until the mid 1970s. Díaz came to

Troilo with impeccable tango training from Carlos Di Sarli. He had met Di Sarli in Bahía Blanca in the mid 1920s, playing with him there ,and later on in his sextet in Buenos Aires. Díaz was always grateful for Di Sarli's generosity and teaching. The occasional violin lead that is heard in Troilo tracks can safely be assumed to be David Díaz. Listen to:

Yo Soy El Tango (1941)

David's brother Enrique (known as Kicho) was not one of those overlooked, under-rated bass players. He was acknowledged then, and is remembered now, as the powerhouse of the Troilo orchestra from its inception up to 1959, providing the rolling, rumbling base that keeps the dancers' feet grounded down into the floor. Afterwards he played and recorded with Piazzolla, including on Pizzolla's tribute composition to him, *Kicho*.

Other than Piazzolla the most well known musician in the orchestra was the pianist Orlando Goñi. He joined Troilo in 1937 and recorded some seventy tracks until he left in 1943 (or more precisely, until he was dismissed for his increased tendency to arrive drunk for performances or not to arrive at all). Goñi's talent was not dissimilar to Biagi's, characterised by playing from the soul and improvising. Troilo's musical arrangers never bothered to include the vitally important piano parts because Goñi would not, or could not, adhere to them; and anyway, they knew that they could not improve upon Goñi's creative contribution. His genius in music was paired with chaos in the rest of his life. He was an uncontrollable gambler, drinker and drug taker. He was never going to live long, and his body gave up in 1945, aged only thirty-one. But his contribution is everywhere in those first and finest Troilo years. Listen to his omnipresence in:

   * *El Tamango* (1941)

Troilo Summary

- Slow and soulful bandoneonist
- Contrasts choppy with smooth
- Changes tempo
- Brought out the best in his singer Fiorentino

APPENDICES

Appendix 1. Playlist: Recommended Listening

TRACKS	YOUR NOTES
CANARO	
Organito de la tarde (1925)	
Duelo Criollo (1939)	
Sin Rumbo (1931)	
Te Quiero Todavía (1939)	
Recuerdos de Paris (1937)	
Corazón Encadenado (1942)	
Alma Tanguera (1927)	
Canto Por No Llorar (1931)	
Todo Te Nombra (1939)	
El Adiós (1938)	
Cuartito Azul (1939)	
La Melodía de Nuestro Adiós (1947)	
Invierno (1937)	
Loca (1938)	
LOMUTO	
Tormenta (Lomuto & Canaro 1939)	
La Gayola (1941)	
Madreselva (1938)	
La Melodía de Nuestro Adiós (1938)	
Nostalgias (1936)	

Appendix 1. Playlist: Recommended Listening

DONATO	
El Acomodo (1933)	
Tierrita (1934)	
Alas Rotas (1938)	
Carnaval de Mi Barrio (1939)	
El Adiós (1938)	
Mendocina (1942)	
Sacale Punta (1938)	
OTV	
El Chamuyo (1930)	
Jueves (1934)	
Adiós Buenos Aires (1938)	
Bajo El Cono Azul (1944)	
Hembra (1928)	
Vieja Calesita (1929)	
FIRPO	
Pablo (1927)	
Desconsuelo (1936)	
No Quiero Verte Llorar (1937)	
La Trilla (1936)	
El Moro (1937)	
Artedecer Campero (1936)	
El Esquinazo (1936)	

Appendix 1. Playlist: Recommended Listening

D'ARIENZO	
Chirusa (1928, 1940 & 1958)	
El Flete (1936)	
La Morocha (1937)	
Dime Mi Amor (1941)	
Don Juan (1950)	
La Puñalada (1937)	
Mandria (1939)	
La Cumparsita (1943)	
BIAGI	
Bélgica (1942)	
Lucienne (1946)	
Gólgota (1938)	
Dichas Que Vivi (1939)	
Humillación (1941)	
Adiós Te Vas (1943)	
Paloma (1945)	
Alguien (1956)	
TANTURI	
Comparsa Criollo (1941)	
El Buey Solo (1941)	
Pocas Palabras (1941)	
Asi Se Baila El Tango (1942)	

La Abandoné y No Sabía (1944)	
Remembranza (1947)	
RODRIGUEZ	
Danza Maligna (1940)	
Tengo Mil Novias (1939)	
Son Cosas del Bandoneón (1939)	
En La Buena y En La Mala (1940)	
Yo No Se Porque Razon (1942)	
MALERBA	
Noches de Montmartre (1941)	
Oiga, Mozo (1942)	
Gitana Rusa (1942)	
Encuentro (1944)	
FRESEDO	
Fumando Espero (1927)	
Isla de Capri (1935)	
Como Aquella Princesa (1937)	
Ronda de Ases (1942)	
Nostalgias (1952)	
Niebla de la Riachuelo (1937)	
Más Allá (1939)	
Alas (1940)	

Appendix 1. Playlist: Recommended Listening

Jamás Retornarás (1943)	
Buscándote (1941)	
DI SARLI	
El Paladin (1929)	
Corazón (1939)	
Ensueños (1943)	
Champagne Tango (1953)	
Bahía Blanca (1957)	
Don José Maria (1943 and 1954)	
Indio Manso (1958)	
Cicatrices (1930)	
Chau Pinela (1930)	
Junto a Tu Corazón (1942)	
Tu!...El Cielo y Tu! (1944)	
Porteño y Bailarín (1945)	
Verdemar (1953)	
Nido Gaucho (1955)	
CALO	
Tarareando (Caló & Di Sarli 1942)	
Al Compás del Corazón (1942)	
Verdemar (1943 Caló & Di Sarli)	
Nada (1944 Caló & Di Sarli)	
Cosas de Tango (Caló 1945, Di Sarli 1946)	

Tristezas de la Calle Corrientes (1942)

Corazón No Le Hagas Caso (1942)

Nada (1944 Caló & Di Sarli)

DEMARE

Un Tango Guapo (1942)

Al Compás de un Tango (1942)

Y Siempre Igual (1943)

No Te Apures, Cara Blanca (1942)

D'AGOSTINO

Adiós Arrabal (1941)

Tres Esquinas (1941)

El Cornetín del Tranvía (1944)

DE ANGELIS

Soy Un Arlequin (1945)

La Vida Me Engañó (1946)

Pregonera (1945)

Remolino (1946)

Pastora (1948)

Tu Intimo Secreto (1955)

Mi Novia de Ayer (1944)

Jirón Porteño (1946)

Mocosita (1949)

Appendix 1. Playlist: Recommended Listening

Bajo El Cono Azul (1944)	
Buenos Aires de Ayer (1943)	
De Igual A Igual (1944)	
DE CARO	
Vayan Saliendo (1928)	
Tierra Negra (1940)	
Tierra Querida (1952)	
De Contrapunto (1936)	
Mi Dolor (1950)	
Esta Noche de Luna (1951)	
El Taita (Raza Criollo) (1928)	
LAURENZ	
Arrabal (1937)	
Nunca Tuvo Novio (1943)	
Mendocina (1944)	
PUGLIESE	
La Yumba (1946)	
Derecho Viejo (1945)	
Amurado (1944)	
Remembranza (1956)	
Farol (1943)	
Una Vez (1946)	
Un Baile de Beneficio (1950)	

Appendix 1. Playlist: Recommended Listening

Cascabelito (1955)	
TROILO	
Comme Il Faut (1938)	
El Tamango (1941)	
Milongueando en el Cuarenta (1941)	
En Esta Tarde Gris (1941)	
No Te Apures, Cara Blanca (1942)	
Tal Vez Sera Tu Voz (1943)	
Yuyo Verde (1945)	
Yo Soy El Tango (1941)	

Appendix 2. Orchestra Leaders' Birth Years and Recording Years

The two tables below present the first and last date of tango recordings by the orchestra leaders. They are intended to give a contextual perspective of how the orchestras fit together chronologically. The tables do not show any intervening breaks from recording (of which there were many).

It is clear that the music that we dance to today represents only a small part of the discography of our twenty orchestras. We should also recognise that all of the orchestras (except for OTV) performed in clubs and cabarets, and on radio, for more years than their recording life. Furthermore, the tracks that they recorded only represent a part of their performing repertoire – numerous performed tangos will remain unknown to us.

Appendix 2. Orchestra Leaders' Birth and Recording Years

Table A: Ordered by Year of Birth:

Born	Orchestra Leader	Recording
1884	Roberto Firpo	1914 – 1961
1888	Francisco Canaro	1915 – 1962
1893	Francisco Lomuto	1926 – 1950
1893	Adolfo Carabelli (OTV)	1932 – 1935
1897	Edgardo Donato	1929 – 1961
1897	Osvaldo Fresedo	1919 – 1968
1899	Julio De Caro	1924 – 1953
1900	Juan D'Arienzo	1928 – 1975
1900	Angel D'Agostino	1940 – 1963
1901	Enrique Rodríguez	1937 – 1971
1902	Pedro Laurenz	1937 – 1969
1903	Luis Petrucelli (OTV)	1925 – 1931
1903	Carlos Di Sarli	1928 – 1958
1905	Ricardo Tanturi	1937 – 1965
1905	Ricardo Malerba	1941 – 1957
1905	Osvaldo Pugliese	1943 – 1986
1905	Mario Maurano (OTV)	1943 – 1944
1906	Rodolfo Biagi	1938 – 1962
1906	Lucio Demare	1938 – 1959
1907	Miguel Caló	1932 – 1972
1910	Alfredo De Angelis	1943 – 1985
1912	Federico Scorticati (OTV)	1936 – 1941
1914	Aníbal Troilo	1938 – 1971

Appendix 2. Orchestra Leaders' Birth and Recording Years

Table B: Ordered by Recording Years:

Recording Span	Orchestra Leader	Born
1914 – 1961	Roberto Firpo	1884
1915 – 1962	Francisco Canaro	1888
1919 – 1968	Osvaldo Fresedo	1897
1924 – 1953	Julio De Caro	1899
1925 – 1931	Luis Petrucelli (OTV)	1903
1926 – 1950	Francisco Lomuto	1893
1928 – 1958	Carlos Di Sarli	1903
1928 – 1975	Juan D'Arienzo	1900
1929 – 1961	Edgardo Donato	1897
1932 – 1935	Adolfo Carabelli (OTV)	1893
1932 – 1972	Miguel Caló	1907
1936 – 1941	Federico Scorticati (OTV)	1912
1937 – 1965	Ricardo Tanturi	1905
1937 – 1969	Pedro Laurenz	1902
1937 – 1971	Enrique Rodríguez	1901
1938 – 1959	Lucio Demare	1906
1938 – 1962	Rodolfo Biagi	1906
1938 – 1971	Aníbal Troilo	1914
1940 – 1963	Angel D'Agostino	1900
1941 – 1957	Ricardo Malerba	1905
1943 – 1944	Mario Maurano (OTV)	1905
1943 – 1985	De Angelis, Alfredo	1910
1943 – 1986	Osvaldo Pugliese	1905

Appendix 3: Orchestra Leaders' Instruments

All the orchestra leaders were musicians, but not all of them played their instruments during their recording years. This table shows what instruments the leaders played, and which leaders played their instruments in their orchestras as well as conducting.

	Orchestra Leader	Instrument	Played
Simple	Canaro	Violin	No
	Lomuto	Piano	No
	Donato	Violin	Yes
	OTV: Petrucelli	Bandoneón	Yes
	OTV: Carabelli	Piano	Yes
	OTV: Scorticati	Bandoneón	Yes
	OTV: Maurano	Piano	Yes
	Firpo	Piano	Yes
Rhythmic	D'Arienzo	Violin	No
	Biagi	Piano	Yes
	Tanturi	Piano	No
	Rodríguez	Bandoneón	No

Appendix 3. Orchestra Leaders' Instruments

	Orchestra Leader	Instrument	Played
	Malerba	Bandoneón	No
Lyrical	Fresedo	Bandoneón	Yes
	Di Sarli	Piano	Yes
	Caló	Bandoneón	No
	Demare	Piano	Yes
	D'Agostino	Piano	Yes
	De Angelis	Piano	Yes
Complex	De Caro	Violin	Yes
	Laurenz	Bandoneón	Yes
	Pugliese	Piano	Yes
	Troilo	Bandoneón	Yes

Appendix 4: Bibliography

Books	
Tango Stories: Musical Secrets	Michael Lavocah
Tango Masters: Anibal Troilo	Michael Lavocah
Mis Memorias	Francisco Canaro
El Senor con Alma de Nino	Girolandini, Biondo, Valle
La Historia del Tango series	published by Corregidor
La Historia del Tango Volumes 1 to 3	Daus, Pujol Baulenas
Nueva Historia del Tango	Hector Benedetti
Mujeres y Hombres Que Hicieron el Tango	José Gobello
El Tango Su Historia y Evolucion	Horacio Ferrer
Historia de la Orquesta Típica	Luis Adolfo Sierra
Buenos Aires Tango Historia	Oscar Fernandez
Breve Historia del Tango	Andres Carretero
Tango: The Art History of Love	Robert Farris Thompson
Encyclopedia of Tango	Gabriel Valiente
The Film Industry in Argentina	Jorge Finkelman
El Tango	Horacio Salas
Magazines	
Los Grandes del Tango	Editorial Tango
Idolos del Espectaculo Argentino series	published by Clarin
Revista La Milonga Argentina series	Silvia Rojas

Appendix 4. Bibliography

Todo Es Historia	Felix Luna
El Firulete series	Planet Tango
Essays	
Doce Ventanas al Tango	Fundacion El Libro
El Tango Un Motivo Sentimental	Ernesto J Abalsamo
Cronicas de Tango	Ernesto J Abalsamo
TV Series & DVDs	
Los Misterios del Tango	paralelo35
La Historia de las Orquestas series	TV Channel 'Volver'
La Historia de los Cantores	TV Channel 'Volver'
El Bandoneón y sus Interpretes	TV Channel 'Volver'
Los Capos del Tango series	Solo Tango
Websites	
www.todotango.com	*www.me.gov.ar/*
www.tangosalbardo.com	*www.vocesdelapatria grande.com*
www.clarin.com	*www.learntangomusic. com*
www.investigaciontango.com	*https://tangoinfo.com*